# Working with F

SKILLS FOR CONTEMPORARY SOCIAL WORK SERIES

Tony Evans and Mark Hardy, *Evidence and Knowledge for Practice*
Andrew Hill, *Working in Statutory Contexts*
Hazel Kemshall, Bernadette Wilkinson and Kerry Baker, *Working with Risk*

# Working with Risk
## Skills for Contemporary Social Work

HAZEL KEMSHALL, BERNADETTE WILKINSON
AND KERRY BAKER

polity

First published in 2013 by Polity Press

Polity Press
65 Bridge Street
Cambridge CB2 1UR, UK

Polity Press
350 Main Street
Malden, MA 02148, USA

ISBN-13: 978-0-7456-5197-2
ISBN-13: 978-0-7456-5198-9(pb)

A catalogue record for this book is available from the British Library.

Typeset in 10.5 on 12 pt Sabon
by Toppan Best-set Premedia Limited
Printed and bound in Great Britain by Clays Ltd, St Ives plc

The publisher has used its best endeavours to ensure that the URLs for external websites referred to in this book are correct and active at the time of going to press. However, the publisher has no responsibility for the websites and can make no guarantee that a site will remain live or that the content is or will remain appropriate.

Every effort has been made to trace all copyright holders, but if any have been inadvertently overlooked the publisher will be pleased to include any necessary credits in any subsequent reprint or edition.

For further information on Polity, visit our website: www.politybooks.com

# Contents

Figures and Activity Boxes                                          vi
Acknowledgements                                                    ix

1   Understanding Risk                                               1

2   Skills for Risk Assessment                                       9

3   The Art of Decision Making                                      43

4   Risk Planning and Management                                    71

5   Risk and Ethics                                                101

6   Review and Evaluation of Risk                                  121

7   Managing Self in the Organizational Context                    146

Conclusion                                                         166

References                                                         173
Index                                                              188

# Figures and Activity Boxes

## Figures

| 1.1 | The cycle of working with risk | 6 |
| 2.1 | Interacting risk factors | 27 |
| 4.1 | Strength of interactions between risk factors | 81 |
| 4.2 | Model of combined risk strategies and gaps | 84 |
| 6.1 | Serious incident review cycles | 129 |
| 6.2 | Framework of knowledge and organizational commitment | 142 |
| 7.1 | The iceberg model | 158 |
| 7.2 | Accountability, reflection and learning, and best practice | 162 |

## Activity Boxes

| 2.1 | Holding the Balance between Risk Avoidance and Positive Risk Taking | 10 |
| 2.2 | Being Clear About the Purpose of Risk Assessment | 12 |
| 2.3 | Benefits and Harms | 16 |
| 2.4 | Supporting Defensible Decision Making | 19 |
| 2.5 | Evaluating an Assessment Procedure | 23 |
| 2.6 | Risk Factors and Causation | 27 |
| 2.7 | Self-Reflection: Strengths and Areas for Development | 30 |
| 2.8 | Planning an Assessment | 32 |
| 2.9 | Communication | 35 |
| 2.10 | Observing and Analysing Practice | 37 |

| | | |
|---|---|---|
| 2.11 | Reflecting on an Interview | 38 |
| 2.12 | The Quality of Information | 39 |
| 2.13 | Returning to Your Attributes and Skills | 41 |
| 3.1 | Considering Ambiguous Factors | 46 |
| 3.2 | Testing Information Sources | 47 |
| 3.3 | Case Study Exercise | 52 |
| 3.4 | Case Study Exercise and Reflection | 54 |
| 3.5 | Testing Inductive Hypotheses on Risk | 56 |
| 3.6 | Reflective Exercise: Negative Emotions and Risk Assessment | 59 |
| 3.7 | Reflective Exercise: Balancing Risk Decisions | 61 |
| 3.8 | Dealing with Risk Dilemmas | 62 |
| 3.9 | Exercise on Bias | 64 |
| 4.1 | Thresholds and Categorization | 74 |
| 4.2 | Balancing Risk Reduction against Potential Negative Outcomes | 76 |
| 4.3 | Balances in Risk-Management Plans | 78 |
| 4.4 | Different Kinds of Risk Factors | 80 |
| 4.5 | Thinking about the Strengths and Directions of Influence | 81 |
| 4.6 | Layers of Risk Strategies | 85 |
| 4.7 | Writing Approach Goals | 88 |
| 4.8 | 'Means–End Thinking' | 90 |
| 4.9 | Footsteps to Change | 93 |
| 4.10 | Scenario Planning | 94 |
| 4.11 | Remembering the Potential for Positive Change | 95 |
| 4.12 | Reading Case Records | 97 |
| 4.13 | Agency and Practitioner Perspectives in Risk Meetings | 99 |
| 5.1 | Case Study | 104 |
| 5.2 | My Own Ethical Beliefs | 107 |
| 5.3 | The Challenges of Rationing | 112 |
| 5.4 | Threats to Personal and Professional Integrity | 113 |
| 5.5 | Can I Lie to You? | 114 |
| 5.6 | Challenge and Reporting | 116 |
| 5.7 | Risk Avoidance and Risk Aversion | 118 |
| 6.1 | Reflective Exercise on Opportunities for Learning | 122 |
| 6.2 | Responding to Recommendations | 127 |
| 6.3 | Organizational Responses to Serious Incidents | 128 |
| 6.4 | Learning from Recurring Problems | 130 |

| | | |
|---|---|---|
| 6.5 | Knowledge of your Local Risk Policy | 133 |
| 6.6 | Testing Fitness for Purpose | 133 |
| 6.7 | Identifying What You Need to Know | 135 |
| 6.8 | Case Studies | 137 |
| 6.9 | Asking the Unasked Questions | 139 |
| 6.10 | Improving System Oversight | 141 |
| 7.1 | Your Own Characteristics | 147 |
| 7.2 | Using Critical Reflection | 149 |
| 7.3 | Your Personal Efficacy Beliefs and Their Effects | 151 |
| 7.4 | Managing Stress | 154 |
| 7.5 | Using Self-Management Skills 1 | 156 |
| 7.6 | Using Self-Management Skills 2 | 157 |
| 7.7 | What is Happening 'Under the Surface' | 158 |
| 7.8 | Informal Discussions | 160 |
| 7.9 | Making the Most of Supervision | 161 |
| 7.10 | Making the Most of Learning Opportunities | 163 |
| 7.11 | Strategies for Self-Management in the Organization | 164 |
| 8.1 | Achieving 'Balanced' Practice | 168 |
| 8.2 | Reflection | 172 |

# Acknowledgements

We would like to thank all the people who have helped with this book, including those who have participated in our training over the years, students and staff of social work courses who have tried some of this material, and staff at the University of the West of Scotland who provided a number of activities. Our thanks also go to Katie Heaton, team leader at Warwick Children and Families Services, for comment and ideas. Thanks also to Kath Hammersley at De Montfort University for formatting and improving the manuscript.

We would like to extend heartfelt thanks to our families and friends who have provided encouragement and support and who have helped us to complete this book. Thanks also to the staff at Polity, including a very patient Jonathan Skerrett who was very kind about deadlines.

# 1

# *Understanding Risk*

Risk assessment and management are core issues in social work across a range of settings and contexts. Responding to the risks posed by others, reducing risks to vulnerable persons and managing risks to themselves are all in a day's work for busy practitioners. Managers and practitioners are routinely confronted with risk decisions, and such decisions are often central to the allocation of resources or the choice of interventions (Kemshall 2002a). Risk is a complex practice issue, and there are different views on the nature of risk, and how to assess and manage it effectively. This chapter will explore the nature of risk, the historical roots of risk as a concept and how it is best understood for those working in social work.

## What is Risk?

Risk has been called the 'world's largest industry' (Adams 1995: 31). We are faced with a bewildering array of risks in our everyday lives, ranging from health risks due to eating the 'wrong foods' to flood risks caused by climatic change. We are constantly told about such risks through the media, and constantly urged to be more aware and to 'manage' risk. At the turn of the century, one journalist expressed our preoccupation with risk in the headline: 'Warning: You're Risking Death by Being Alive' (Thomson 2000: 21). Thomson painted the twenty-first century as a risky place, noting risks to newborn babies arising from their mothers' kisses, to vaccines, to cot death, food risks and paedophile abductions on the way to school. As she put it, being a mother is a risky business, and 'every day there is another reason to worry.' Some risks we choose to accept (those associated with travel are readily accepted as the 'price' we pay for moving around); some risks we actively seek (like gambling or bungee jumping for the thrill); some we seek to avoid (like becoming the victim of crime). Other risks are beyond our personal control, for example those associated with nuclear power plant discharge, such as the Fukushima disaster in Japan, or acid rain. These are risks emanating from far away and often caused by others we do not know or control, or by the failure of regulatory systems set up to protect us.

The word 'risk' can also have different meanings. To some 'risk' means thrill, or the chance of gaining a reward for minimum effort (gambling), and risk-taking is an acknowledged and usually valued feature of entrepreneurship and venture capital (Higgs 1931), at least until the excesses of the global financial crisis of 2008. Increasingly, however, 'risk' has been linked to danger, peril and hazard (*Oxford English Dictionary* 2012) and used almost entirely with negative connotations. One consequence of this has been a developing culture of risk aversion (Power 2004), reflected in a precautionary or 'better safe than sorry' approach to risk. This in turn can lead to defensive practice, and organizational cultures that are focused on risk avoidance and blame.

The framing of risk as danger has a long history, and the English term 'risk' came into common usage in the seventeenth century with the development of marine insurance. The rise of the slave trade and the extensive shipment of cotton led to formal calculations of safety levels on shipping routes, in effect calculating whether a ship was likely to return to port safely or not and insuring appropriately against any loss (Kemshall 2003). Lloyd's of London famously started this business, and utilized statistics, especially on death rates and shipping losses, to produce actuarial tables of risk (Hacking 1987). The insurance industry still operates in this way today. In 1762, Equitable Life set up the first life insurance and again drew on actuarial tables of death rates across the population as a whole to ensure calculations of life expectancy; life insurance policies were calculated and costed accordingly. The Napoleonic Wars saw further interest in life insurance, particularly for 'soldiers of fortune' selling their services. Many came from Scotland, and life assurance was sought for the widows and orphans that might be left behind. The company we now know as Scottish Widows has its roots in this era. By the nineteenth century, insurance was a common industry, and the notion of risk as a probability calculation based on tables of data was firmly embedded (Hacking 1987, 1990). Probability and therefore prediction of risk were linked; risk could be known and assessed if only the right tools were used (Daston 1987).

The late nineteenth and early twentieth century saw the extension of insurance and probability calculations of risk into social life. For example, mutual societies enabled the working man to insure against accident or illness, and such societies were common in coal mining areas, extending later into many areas of industrial life. The Co-operative Society was one of the largest mutual societies and has its roots in the heavy industries of the north of England. The notion of pooling resources to deal with individual risks of misfortune was strongly embedded in the British welfare state for much of the twentieth century, and across other anglophone nations (Kemshall 2003). Personal risks and misfortune were not merely a matter for the individual, but were seen as part of the collective state response, for example through welfare benefits for those too ill to work.

By the late twentieth and early twenty-first centuries, actuarial or probability calculations of risk had become common across many aspects of social life, and formalized risk assessment tools began to play a key part in assessments of welfare entitlement, in social work, social care and crime management policies (Kemshall 2002b). Interestingly, as techniques for risk assessment improved, the idea of a collective response to individual risks began to wane. The burgeoning costs of welfare across all the anglophone countries resulted in aggressive social policies to reduce the size and responsibilities of the state, a situation given considerable impetus by the global financial crisis of 2008. Risk and responsibility became entwined, with much social policy placing responsibility for assessing and managing risks onto the individual. Personal misfortune became exactly that, and citizens are increasingly expected to foresee and manage their own risks (e.g. saving for old age, insuring against unemployment). In social work, risk has come to predominate as a way of categorizing users, cases and responses, and social work's focus is often on those citizens who are deemed to take risks irresponsibly, or who pose risks to others and therefore require managing (Kemshall 2010a).

## Understanding Risk in Social Work

We are all faced with numerous risk decisions in our personal lives, but professional decisions about risk are different. As Carson and

Bain put it, 'professional risk-taking is undertaken for the benefit of others from a duty to assist them' (2008: 31). This is the underlying imperative for risk decisions in social work.

Risks in social work can be separated into two broad categories:

- those risks which people *pose to others*; and
- those risks to which people are exposed, in other words, people who are *vulnerable* to risk. (Kemshall 2002a: 124)

One of the most obvious social work areas in which people pose a risk to others is in child protection. Parents and other adults may pose a range of risks to children, ranging from physical risks, sexual abuse, neglect and risks arising from particular adult lifestyles, such as alcohol or drug use. In these circumstances, workers will not only focus on the needs of the child but will be concerned to accurately assess the type of risks posed; how likely they are to occur, when and how; and what interventions can be put into place to reduce the risk. In such situations, the rights of the poser of risk can be limited in the interests of protecting others or of preventing further risks.

Assessing vulnerability to risk is equally relevant to a number of service-user groups and to a number of settings, for example, care of older persons, work with vulnerable adults, support for young people leaving care. What is critical to assessments of risk in this area is: a clear focus on the risks the person is exposed to; how they might impact on the person and with what consequences; whether such risks are acceptable or not; what risk reduction strategies can be used and how these might impact on the quality of life and autonomy of the person and with what benefit(s); and how risk management can be balanced with the promotion of autonomy, quality of life and individual rights (Kemshall 2002a: 125).

However, in daily practice, such neat distinctions don't always apply. Some service users will fall into both the categories of posing risk and being at risk. For example, young people leaving care may commit offences and present risk to others, but will also be vulnerable to abuse from older adults, and at risk because of poor accommodation, lack of employment and lack of support and care. A number of high-profile cases have also highlighted the vulnerability of mentally disordered persons who have committed serious offences. The inquiry by Blom-Cooper, Hally and Murphy (1995) identified how failures in community care contributed to the escalation of risk in the case of Andrew Robinson and his subsequent killing of Georgina Robinson. The inquiry noted the failure of treatment, and the failure to respond to Robinson's deteriorating mental health and the concerns of his family and friends. Andrew Robinson had a history of mental illness since 1978 and had been in Broadmoor Special Hospital following a conviction for possession of a firearm with intent to endanger life. Robinson presents as both vulnerable and as a potential poser of risk to others. The case also illustrates how the risks that a person is exposed to can exacerbate the risks they pose to others. In such cases, it is important that the practitioner assess *both* types of risk – if the focus is only on vulnerability, the risks to others are overlooked; if the focus is only on posing a risk to others, then key issues in the person's life will remain unaddressed and these may heighten risk to others over time. Once the practitioner has assessed risk and vulnerability, the important next step is to consider how they interact, what will exacerbate risk and what might mitigate those risks.

Addressing these difficult and challenging risk issues is the focus of this book. The emphasis is not on risk assessment as a 'tool' or a process, but on risk assessment as a decision and, in many cases, risk assessment as a series of decisions. Complex, significant, life-changing decisions require skill and competence, and acquiring skill and building competence are key themes in this book. While bureaucratic and administrative procedures attempt to 'tame chance' (Hacking 1987), and a plethora of structured risk-assessment tools have been developed, risks are not always assessable through formal probabilistic assessment tools, due to lack of knowledge, and are subject to a number of 'it depends'. Social workers have to operate in a 'climate of uncertainty', in which a proportion of decisions will have poor outcomes. Practitioners have to make decisions in situations of stress and under the spectre of potential blame, and in contexts where service-user views of risk and those of workers may be at odds. As Baker and Wilkinson put it: 'Practitioners and managers are faced with the challenge of making demanding decisions about risk with the added pressures of working in a climate of limited resources and intense media and political scrutiny' (2011: 13). This book aims to help both those training to become social workers, and those already in the profession to make those demanding decisions.

## Structure of the Book

It is no accident that the word 'skills' features in the subtitle of this book. Acquiring skills through reading is of course difficult, and social workers can only improve their practice through practising and reflecting. Through the use of case studies and reflective exercises, this book fosters such an approach. The book attempts to follow the ideal practice journey of risk assessment, formulating risk plans and comparing options, implementing risk-management plans, reassessing and reflecting on impact and outcomes, and revising plans where appropriate. This cycle requires key tasks to be performed, including preparation for the assessment task, information gathering, analysis of what is found, risk-management planning, delivery as intended, and review, all of which should be supported by thorough recording. This is expressed in Figure 1.1.

The book focuses on this critical process, with chapter 2 introducing the assessment procedures, with an emphasis on purposeful information gathering and in-depth analysis. Chapter 3 looks at the exercise of 'good judgement' and argues that informed, balanced and critical reasoning are essential to sound decision making. The pitfalls of risk-decision making, for example those created by bias and discrimination, are explored, and challenging risk decisions are also recognized as ones which can lead to defensive practice. Chapter 4 examines risk planning and management and argues that effective plans must flow from a balanced, evidence-based risk assessment. Importantly, the chapter focuses attention on the identification of desirable risk reduction outcomes, and how planning must demonstrate how these are likely to be achieved. Plans also have to be

**Figure 1.1**  The cycle of working with risk

delivered and reviewed, but rightly the chapter encourages readers to consider the requirement for flexibility in the light of change and the dynamic nature of risk. Contingency planning and mechanisms for monitoring implementation are required, and plans require review in order to establish that they are working and delivering desirable outcomes.

Risk assessment and management also present key dilemmas and challenges for social workers. These are areas of work particularly prone to ethical dilemmas and can present tensions between 'social control, social care, social justice and social change' (Barry 2009: 111). Chapter 5 examines a range of such tensions and likely challenges for social workers and presents a number of exercises to encourage the reader to rehearse and reflect on how such challenges can be faced and resolved. The discussion is informed by contemporary ethical codes in social work, but the limits of such codes in resolving real-life ethical dilemmas are acknowledged.

Review and evaluation of risk management is critical, but this can involve more than the review of individual plans. Chapter 6 locates review and evaluation within the wider context of risk policies, procedures and systems, and looks at the role of managers as well as practitioners in delivering effective and balanced risk management. Learning from both good practice and risk failures is seen as critical for improving performance, and the chapter also examines how quality assurance can be improved.

Decisions about risk also take place under conditions of uncertainty. We can never truly know all there is to know, and decisions do not take place under ideal conditions (for example, there are almost always time pressures and resource constraints). These conditions can often make us feel anxious and stressed. It is therefore important that we can manage these impacts on ourselves, and chapter 7 examines in some detail how best to 'manage self' within the demanding organizational context of social work. Reflective practice is seen as one key technique for helping social workers deal with a demanding and stressful job, where blame is often only one decision away. To assist readers with critical reflection, the reader is invited to engage with a range of activities, case studies and reflective exercises throughout the book. These can be used on social work training courses, in work settings to review practice, and with social work teams for staff development. Where relevant, feedback is provided, and activities are boxed and numbered for ease of access.

Finally, the conclusion recognizes that risk decisions are often life-changing ones and seeks to reiterate a number of key themes and good practice messages from the book. Working positively with risk, and in an informed and balanced manner, is seen as critical. This book does not have all the answers, but aims to help social work practitioners to make positive, thoughtful, robust and ethical decisions about risk.

# 2

# *Skills for Risk Assessment*

Risk assessment is not an end in itself; however, it must be purposeful. Figure 1.1 made clear that information gathering and analysis at the outset of any case should guide service delivery. As planned-for services are delivered, the impact of any actions taken (and of actions not pursued) should be reviewed, contributing to a developing picture and often necessitating new information gathering and analysis.

This purposeful risk-assessment practice will be built on a range of interrelated and mutually dependent skills and knowledge, including the practical use, in context, of relevant legislation and policy. Communication skills are important for example, but effective communication may also require skills in managing conflict and challenge (Keys 2009b), so that again the practical application of skills in context is central.

So how effectively have relevant risk-assessment skills and knowledge been applied in social work and if not always effectively, why not? There have been well-documented and publicized concerns about the effectiveness of the risk-assessment and management process in social work, particularly in relation to child protection (Laming 2003, 2009) and for those working with the mentally ill (NHS London 2006). While the hope is always that inquiries and investigations into practice will improve outcomes, they have not always had the intended effect. Responses by commentators and policy makers can be polarized; for example, Maden (2011) suggests that the debate about violence and mental health has been characterized by extremes, with focus on assaults by the mentally ill and concerns about their human rights being unhelpfully seen as mutually exclusive. Practitioners will find it harder to exercise skills with confidence if they are struggling to locate their work in a very politicized and polarized context. Responses to inquiries can be bureaucratic and procedural in nature (Reder and Duncan 2004a) and are also influenced by considerations of resource management with sometimes conflicting demands on the available and limited resources (Davies 2008). This has contributed to an organizational focus on procedures, with less attention paid to the skills and understandings that are essential, whatever the procedural basis of practice (Brandon, Dodsworth and Rumball 2005; Keys 2009a, b; Munro 2011). 'The focus on work with risk becomes data storage and communicating risk, with less attention to service-user engagement or to risk management itself' (Kemshall 2010a: 1255).

Given the climate of scrutiny of risk decisions in modern society, it is perhaps unsurprising that discussions tend to focus on risk avoidance: the attempt to prevent harm occurring by identifying and tackling those risk factors which increase the likelihood of a harmful event. It is important at the outset, however, to emphasize that effective work with people doesn't just involve the avoidance of risk but also requires the taking of positive risks to support personal growth and development (McDonald 2010a; Titterton 2011). Manthorpe and Moriarty (2010: 8) talk about risk enablement: 'the process of measuring risk involves balancing the positive benefits from taking risks against the negative effects of attempting to avoid risk altogether.' Risk assessment needs to look for and find opportunities to build on the resilience and strengths in individuals and situations. The skills utilized in risk assessment therefore include skills in holding the balance between planned and purposeful risk taking and risk avoidance.

---

### Activity 2.1   Holding the Balance between Risk Avoidance and Positive Risk Taking

To think this balance through, consider an example from everyday life. Parents have to decide, bearing in mind the age and characteristics of their child and the circumstances in which the family lives, what degree of freedom of movement is appropriate.

1   Make a general list of the potential benefits of allowing a child of, let's say, 10 years old increased unsupervised outdoor play.
2   List the potential risks of that same unsupervised outdoor play.

3  Identify strengths that would make it easier to take positive risks.
4  Identify risk factors that would make you more cautious.

What lessons can you learn from this for risk assessment in social work?

## The Focus of Risk Assessment

'Risk assessment' is now a frequently heard phrase but it is important to think carefully about the language that is being used and what terms like this actually mean in practice. Risk assessment includes a consideration of two key elements (Carson and Bain 2008):

- the likelihood of an event occurring;
- the extent of harm or benefit involved in any potential outcome.

In addition, risk assessment includes a consideration of the imminence of a harmful event. Confusion can arise if risk assessors are not clear about all of those elements and how they interrelate with each other. Any discussion of risk must also recognize that decisions about future likelihood and harm or benefits are not certain; assessors have to live with uncertainty and this is an intrinsic feature of the risk-assessment process.

### Purpose

Based on this understanding of the nature of risk – its key components and inherent uncertainty – the basic purpose of risk assessment in individual cases, therefore, should be clearly understood as:

- identifying what risks are being considered to whom and why, being specific about the behaviour(s) or event(s) of concern;
- calculating the likelihood or probability that the behaviour or event in question will occur and considering its imminence, that is, how soon it is likely to happen;
- estimating the likely impact and consequences of the behaviour or event in question and on whom;
- identifying the circumstances and conditions that increase or decrease likelihood and/or impact.

Before you go on to read the rest of the chapter, you may want to use the following activity to help you consider your own practice and to inform your subsequent reading.

---

**Activity 2.2   Being Clear About the Purpose of Risk Assessment**

This table could be used in supervision to structure a discussion about a case. It could also be used in teaching and training to structure small group discussions about a case study. If you are currently practising, use this table to have a discussion with a colleague or a supervisor about a current risk assessment.

| |
|---|
| Who is at risk and why? Be specific. |
| How likely is the event or behaviour you have identified to happen? |
| How imminent do you think it is? |
| If it does happen what will the likely impact be? |
| Make a note of any circumstances that will make the event more likely or the impact more serious. |

---

Practitioners who are unsure about what they are seeking to achieve, and why, are sometimes part of decision-making processes that fail to protect vulnerable children and other victims of violence or neglect (Laming 2003). Being clear why you are gathering, analysing and recording information is essential for making good quality decisions.

### Individuals and contexts: different risks and their effects

To achieve this clarity of purpose, practitioners need to be precise and specific as they consider each of the elements listed above. As they are doing so in a range of working contexts, they will also require knowledge about different groups of service users, about specific working contexts and about the context within which the risk may occur. For example, if you are concerned with risks to older people, this may involve risk within their own home, sometimes from members of their own family, or it may involve risks in care homes from members of staff.

So what is under consideration when assessing risk for specific groups of service users? The World Health Organization (2002: 126) quotes this definition of elder abuse: 'Elder abuse is a single or repeated act, or lack of appropriate action, occurring within any relationship where there is an expectation of trust which causes harm or distress to an older person.' Note that abuse may arise through action or inaction.

This initial definition can be expanded in relation to older people by identifying a range of abuse types:

- physical abuse – the infliction of pain or injury, physical coercion, or physical or drug-induced restraint;
- psychological or emotional abuse – the infliction of mental anguish;
- financial or material abuse – the illegal or improper exploitation or use of funds or resources of the older person;
- sexual abuse – non-consensual sexual contact of any kind with the older person;
- neglect – the refusal or failure to fulfil a care giving obligation. This may or may not involve a conscious and intentional attempt to inflict physical or emotional distress on the older person. (WHO 2002: 1270)

Equivalent definitions can be given for other areas of practice; for example, the DCSF (2010: 38) offers this definition of abuse and neglect of children: 'Abuse and neglect are forms of maltreatment of a child. Somebody may abuse or neglect a child by inflicting harm, or by failing to act to prevent harm. Children may be abused in a family or in an institutional or community setting, by those known to them or, more rarely, by a stranger, for example, via the internet. They may be abused by an adult or adults, or another child or children.' Munro (2011) reminds us that vulnerability to abuse will vary across individuals, depending in part on the characteristics of the child; for example, babies and teenagers having different needs and experiences.

For any working context, practitioners need to have knowledge therefore not only of the range of risks they are considering, but also of the potential *impact* of those risks on victims. A consideration of the emotional abuse of children includes age or developmentally inappropriate expectations being placed on them (DCSF 2010). A child protection worker would need to understand how children develop healthily and safely in order to make judgements about signs of inappropriate expectations and how serious their impact is likely to be. They would, in addition, need to have some understanding of context to support a judgement about the likely impact on a given individual.

While a single event may cause such harm, more usually it is a compilation of events 'both acute and longstanding, which interrupt, change, or damage the child's physical and psychological development' (DCSF 2010: 36). They suggest that assessors should consider the nature of the harm and its impact, special needs and parental capacity and the context of the family and wider environment. In working with adults, similar specialist understandings are needed, for example when working with a vulnerable adult with communication difficulties (Pritchard 2008).

It can be difficult for practitioners to be confident in making judgements if there is a lack of clarity or agreement about what is meant by significant harm. For example, practitioners may find it hard to make judgements about the extent of harm arising from long-lasting neglect. Practitioners may worry that they are making value judgements, for example, about standards of child care, but need to have a focus not just on health and safety risks for children, but also on the child's lived experience. For example, if a child is smelly and dirty, how does that affect friendships and normal development? 'Abuse and neglect rarely present with a clear, unequivocal picture. It is often the totality of information, the overall pattern of the child's story that raised suspicions of possible abuse or neglect' (Munro 2011: 79). This quote could equally apply to other groups of service users.

All the examples so far have focused on potential harms. Risk assessment is most usually thought about in terms of bad outcomes and the reduction of risk. Risk reduction can, however, sometimes be achieved by supporting strengths and should be combined with attempts to support positive outcomes and to actively engage service users so that they can play a part themselves in risk management. An understanding of individuals in context must include potential strengths and resilience and the place of positive risk taking (Titterton 2005, 2011). For example, taking risks can be important in helping young people and others learn and develop resilience and in allowing for the retention of independence amongst older people or those with dementia (Bornat and Bytheway 2010; Manthorpe and Moriarty 2010; Boeck and Fleming 2011). Both risk reduction and purposeful risk taking should be focused on outcomes and should include the involvement of, and informed decision making by, service users.

## Holding the balance

This balancing of risk reduction and positive risk taking is just one of the balances taken into account in risk assessment, including:

- weighing risk prevention against the risks posed by intervention, where there may be a lack of clear evidence to support the likely efficacy of different courses of action (Sheppard 2008; Milner and O'Byrne 2009; Davidson-Arad 2010);
- maximizing the well-being of those concerned, while minimizing harm to individuals, or the harm that an individual may pose to others (Munro 2008a);
- balancing taking risks in order to allow the development of strengths and opportunities with the avoidance of the risk of harm;
- balancing intervening in order to reduce risk and improve people's lives with a responsibility to use limited resources wisely;
- balancing role clarity for the practitioner about risk reduction while also sustaining a collaborative approach and engagement with service users;
- balancing individual interventions with interventions targeted at damaging social contexts; balancing prevention with protection (Davies 2008; Carey and Foster 2011).

For example, in different working contexts, protection of individuals and of the public has to be balanced with the rights of older people to autonomy and freedom of action; protection of children balanced with a family's right to privacy; and a proper concern with the risk of violence amongst the mentally ill balanced with the dangers of stigmatizing and unfair restrictions of liberty (McDonald 2010a, b; Maden 2011).

## Activity 2.3   Benefits and Harms

This activity asks you to think about the potential balance of benefits and harms to all those affected by a risk decision. You could apply this thinking to the following case study.

Helen is a single mother of 23, living with her two children, Sam, 5 and Molly, 3. The children are subject to an interim care order. Helen is separated from the children's father who is a chaotic poly-drug misuser. There is a history of domestic violence in their relationship and of the children witnessing that violence, although no suggestion of physical injury to the children. Helen herself has a long-standing history of drug misuse and is currently engaging with a treatment agency and is receiving a script as she recovers from a heroin addiction.

The children were initially allowed to stay with Helen, despite some concerns, because she usually provides them with love and stimulation and meets their physical needs well. The two children are close to each other and clearly attached to their mother. Sam is a quiet boy who wants to please adults around him and who worries about his mum. Molly seems more relaxed and less aware of the difficulties in the family. There have been concerns in the past about Helen neither paying attention to the children, nor cooperating with Sam's school and about there being insufficient money to meet the children's basic needs. There were concerns for their safety and for the abuse they witnessed when their father was in the home. When she is feeling stressed, Helen finds the children add to her feelings of pressure and in the past she has used drugs to cope with those feelings.

The original decision for the children to remain with their mother has been reassessed as there is evidence that Helen, while taking her script, has also used heroin over the last few weeks. She had also resumed contact with their father, although she says that he has not returned to live with them or had any contact with the children. She wasn't honest with staff about these developments. The children's school and nursery had raised concerns that they were arriving late and Helen was sometimes very late in collecting them. They still appeared well cared for but Sam was even quieter than usual and reluctant to part from his mother.

Once presented with these concerns Helen has been willing to re-engage with services and has not been using heroin over the last three weeks. She states that she has ended contact with her ex-partner, realizing that he will only make her life more difficult and that she regrets the relapses. Helen is quite isolated at present and is worried about coping on her own.

It is decided that the children can remain with their mother provided she maintains recent good progress and works closely with all the agencies involved. There will also be a focus on supporting Helen to become less isolated.

Use the following table to list the benefits and harms to key individuals affected by the most recent decision to allow the children to remain with their mum. Complete the table for each of the children and for Helen.

| Decision: | Name: | Name: | Name: | Name: |
|---|---|---|---|---|
| | Benefits: | Benefits: | Benefits: | Benefits: |
| | Harms: | Harms: | Harms: | Harms: |

You could also use this approach to think about a risk decision you need to make at work or on placement. Again, list concerned individuals and the benefits and harms and see if it makes a difference to your decision making.

Risk assessment shouldn't be seen as something that is 'done to' someone. Instead, wherever possible it should be a collaborative enterprise, actively involving the subject or subjects of the assessment 'doing with'. This is important both to ensure that the subject's perspective is heard and incorporated, but also because it is the beginning of establishing a positive basis for a working relationship which will enable risk management. For example, an older child may have been removed from home because of concerns about abuse or neglect, but may resist removal and run away from foster placements. The child's perspective will be an essential component of risk assessment and management, although the difficult decisions will still rest with the practitioner. Barnett and Mann (2011) argue for the incorporation of strengths within risk assessments of sexual offenders to make that assessment a more productive, collaborative process. They suggest that this approach can be balanced with the rigorous consideration of risk to others and that it can make risk assessment more accurate and realistic, in part because it encourages greater disclosure and openness.

The art of balanced practice is also affected by the reality of the political and social context within which it is taking place. Addressing risk factors can have the effect of reducing attention to other needs, particularly when resources are limited. In work with children, there has sometimes been confusion between risk and need and between prevention and protection. Davies (2008) suggests that a preventative agenda has led to a lack of clarity about risk, getting in the way of helping practitioners understand prevention and protection together, rather than in opposition. Risk and need should be defined in terms of each other: 'if a child's needs are not being met, there is a risk of harm. If a child is at risk of abuse then he or she is in danger of not having some needs met' (Munro 2008a). Risk assessment therefore needs to be located within a broader assessment of the child and the family. While policy contexts vary, similar considerations apply to other areas of social work; for example, empowerment, risk and protection are all central in addressing the integrity of older people's lives (McDonald 2010a).

While risk assessments and the goals for intervention that arise from those assessments are often focused on the individual and the family, it is also important to assess and manage risk with an understanding of the social forces impacting on the individuals concerned (France, Freiberg and Homel 2010; Manthorpe et al. 2010). Poverty, poor housing and areas of relatively high deprivation will, for example, affect the lived experiences of those being assessed and make a difference to the approaches to risk reduction that can be put into place.

The personalization agenda for adult service users provides an interesting contemporary example for exploring the challenge of balancing risk taking with risk management in a particular practice and policy context. The National Council on Independent Living (NCIL) states 'disabled people must be given the same rights to take risks as all citizens' (National Council on Independent Living 1999: 8), quoted in Littlechild and Glasby (2011). Allowing individuals to manage their own budgets and to self-direct support brings with it risks and benefits. Views are currently divided about the balance between the two. The NCIL suggests that, as the personalization process develops, it should 'identify ways of helping people focus on the outcomes they wish to achieve, identify the risks involved and help facilitate the means to achieve them in ways that are legal, safe, ethical and reasonable' (Littlechild and Glasby 2011: 169). Carr (2010) uses the term 'risk enablement' to suggest the importance of allowing service users to be enabled to take appropriate risks. She points out, however, that access to choice and control for service users perceived as vulnerable may be compromised by the anxieties of practitioners about risk and their fear of being held accountable.

Access to choice and control may also be compromised by the realities of some service users' living conditions. Best practice will balance risk avoidance with risk taking in assessing and managing risk but 'there is a delicate balance between empowerment and safeguarding, choice and risk. It is important for practitioners to consider when the need for protection would override the decision to promote choice and empowerment' (Department of Health 2007: 30, para. 2.50).

## Defensible Practice

In achieving balanced judgements, practitioners are aiming for defensible practice. Such practice 'intertwines aspects of professionalism (e.g. using knowledge and skills) with issues of procedural compliance' (Baker and Wilkinson 2011: 15). Defensible practice should include the application of:

- appropriate levels of knowledge and skill
- appropriate use of information
- risk assessment grounded in the evidence
- communication with relevant others
- risk-management plan linked to risks and risk level
- risk-management plan delivered with integrity
- all reasonable steps
- collection and thorough evaluation of information
- clear recording. (Kemshall 1997a)

Social work should be supported by procedure but not limited by it. Practitioners should be able to reflect on the balances embedded in risk assessment and decision making, discussed above, to tailor their practice response.

---

**Activity 2.4   Supporting Defensible Decision Making**

You can use the following table to think about defensible decision making in a specific practice context: the place where you work or have worked, or where you have completed a placement, for example.

The example below takes two of the elements of defensible decision making and identifies some procedures that support defensible decision making and some of the knowledge and skills that would be needed to make best use of those procedures. Read the examples and compile your own table adding other examples of procedures and knowledge from your chosen practice context. Then take three other elements of defensible decision making listed above and expand the table.

| Component of defensible decision making | Procedures to support defensible decisions | Knowledge and skills to use those procedures effectively |
|---|---|---|
| Appropriate levels of knowledge and skill. | Supervision and appraisal identifying developmental needs. Regular observed practice. | Being able to reflect on practice. Being able to admit non-defensively areas in which you need to develop. |
| Communication with relevant others. | Service level agreements between agencies, referral or reporting procedures and associated paperwork. | Active listening skills in making accurate notes of conversations. Skills in engagement with service users and families. |

Look back over your thoughts. Are the procedures supporting the use of knowledge and skills appropriate and vice versa? For example, do the recording systems you use allow you to record thoughtfully and is the balance right between recording and spending time engaging with others?

## Approaches to Risk Assessment

Risk assessment and management in social work should be based on structured professional judgement, rooted in a holistic understanding which considers the subject of the assessment both in their family and in a wider context. Structured professional judgement is informed by a range of assessment methods that bring together information derived from our knowledge of groups, with a more personal understanding of each individual, family and context being considered.

### *Actuarial and unstructured clinical assessments*

*Unstructured clinical assessments* are based on the subjective judgement of the assessor. They allow for an individualized and contextualized picture, but are very subject to bias, an element of practice which is covered in depth in the next chapter. Researchers and policy makers have therefore sought to find other approaches to risk assessment to increase accuracy and reliability.

Notwithstanding the difficulties inherent in trying to predict the future, workers are often asked to estimate the likelihood of a particular harmful event occurring in the future. They can draw on *actuarial assessments* that make statistical calculations of probability by estimating an individual's likely behaviour based on the behaviour of other individuals with similar characteristics in similar circumstances (Kemshall 2008a). Actuarial approaches are well developed in some fields, for example in criminal justice, but less well developed in social work. Where they have been developed and properly evaluated, they have been found to be more accurate in prediction than unsupported clinical judgements. However, they have significant limitations:

- as they are based on groups, they don't provide a picture of a particular individual (Beckett 2008; Munro 2008a). The number and type of previous convictions may contribute to an estimate of the likelihood of further offending, but some individuals with the same statistical likelihood will not reoffend, while others with fewer convictions will go on to do so;
- the difficulty lies in predicting the most serious behaviours which occur relatively infrequently (low base rates).

Actuarial assessments rely on risk factors that have been identified through research. An approach to assessment based solely on risk factors is problematic as it:

- leads to an emphasis on negatives and may mean that strengths are not acknowledged;
- means that judgements are limited to those risk factors that have been researched.

A risk factor approach doesn't of itself clarify the difference between correlations and causation. Later in this chapter, we consider risk factors for particular groups of service users. For example, child abuse is statistically more likely amongst teen parents. An assessor would still need to understand how that association operates in practice (Wikström and Treiber 2008). In other words, is being a teen parent directly or indirectly causing the behaviour in question and if so how? This is not to say that knowing about risk factors is not important: it is, but actuarially based approaches can conflict with a rights-based approach to practice (e.g. McDonald 2010b discusses this tension in relation to working with older people experiencing dementia).

### Structured professional judgement and associated assessment tools

Increasingly, therefore, structured assessment tools that combine actuarial elements with structured clinical judgement are being developed, to try and maximize the strengths of the risk factor-based approaches, while minimizing their limitations (Kemshall 2008b; Maden 2011). They sometimes include purely actuarial calculations as part of their overall assessment of risk and are based on the risk factors most well supported by research to guide the thinking and recording of the risk assessor (Debidin 2009; Baker, Kelly and Wilkinson 2011). By using these elements, they allow for greater consistency but also support structured clinical judgements derived from individualized information about how those factors are affecting the individual or family concerned. This makes them better able to inform the detail of planning and they often include planning as part of their structure.

Structured judgement tools are not without their own critics and can have limitations. For example, the Common Assessment Framework (CAF) and its embodiment of assessment practice in information technology as the Integrated Children's System (ICS) have been criticized for emphasizing the gathering of information over the relationship between the practitioner and the family. They are criticized for making it harder for the assessor to see the individual's story and the interaction between numbers of influences on their behaviours (Pithouse et al. 2009; Broadhurst et al. 2010; Peckover et al. 2011). Milner and O'Byrne (2009) suggest that the focus on risk factors narrows the attention of the assessor who pays less attention to other aspects of assessment, including strengths and resilience, and who may find it hard to see the picture of the individual and situation as a whole. Structured tools sometimes also support fragmented practice, reducing the ability of the worker to develop practice expertise; for example, if an initial referral process is carried out by specialist staff who do not do subsequent assessments, their knowledge and expertise will remain restricted, which may limit the development of their ability to pick up important information at the referral stage

(Burton and Van den Broeck 2009). Langan (2009) suggests that, in the context of the computerized records of the mentally ill, triggers and contexts for risk are under-recorded. Similar points have been raised in the context of the assessment of offenders (Craissati and Sindall 2009).

Munro (2011) links debate about assessment frameworks to the proliferation of rules for practice, suggesting they have become too specific, making proportionate assessments more difficult. She calls for a better differentiation between rules and professional guidance, defining the latter as principles that professionals apply intelligently in particular cases. A rule might require a practitioner to complete part of an assessment at a particular point in time; professional guidance might support the importance of speedy decision making, but leave judgements about precise timescales, at least in part, to the professional concerned. People's lives are complex and professional judgement rooted in relationships with service users and others will always be essential. Social workers should seek to use the benefits of a structured approach alongside those that flow from professional insights and understandings (Baker 2005, 2007). The skilful nature of judgement and decision making is explored in more depth in chapter 3.

---

**Activity 2.5   Evaluating an Assessment Procedure**

This activity asks you to evaluate a risk-assessment procedure in social work that you are aware of, ideally a process you have had some experience of using, but it would be equally interesting to try this out on any social work assessment process:

- Can you identify how risk factors drawn from research have led to some or all of the questions?
- In asking the questions and completing the paperwork, is an assessor able to use their professional judgement?
- What aspects did you consider helpful to decision making?
- Is there anything that you feel might interfere with the ability to make a good risk assessment?

Reflecting on all of your answers, to what extent do you feel that risk assessment using this process is governed by procedural rules and to what extent by principles that allowed the assessor to make their own decisions? Is this a helpful balance?

## Risk Factors and Estimating Future Risk

If you completed the activity above, you may have concluded that the process did balance rules and principles. It can be helpful, for example, to be constrained to consider particular areas that have been found to be associated with risk, while at the same time being given some choice about how you engage with that and what you record as a result. Whether or not a structured process is used, practitioners will be making estimations about the likelihood of a range of outcomes as they make assessments in a variety of contexts. To do so, they should take into account those risk factors indicated by research as most closely associated with particular harmful outcomes, whether or not a procedure makes them do so. In relation to abuse of children, or of adults within families, risk factors are those things that are more common in abusive families than in others (Munro 2007, 2008a). Relevant factors follow for a number of groups.

### Risk factors for violence in the mentally ill

Most people who are violent are not mentally ill, and most mentally ill persons are not violent. However, there are predictors for future violence by those who are mentally ill:

- a previous history of violence while mentally ill
- substance misuse
- failure to take medication
- psychopathy and other personality disorders
- negative attitudes and lack of insight (Harvard Mental Health Letter 2011; Maden 2011)

### Risk factors for child abuse

Parent-related:

- history of physical or sexual abuse (as a child)
- teen parents
- single parents
- emotional immaturity, poor coping skills, low self-esteem
- substance abuse
- known past history of child abuse
- male partners with criminal histories

- lack of social support (community and extended family)
- domestic violence
- lack of parenting skills
- lack of preparation for the stress of a new infant
- depression or other mental illnesses
- multiple young children
- situations where child access is a factor

Child-related:

- prematurity
- disability
- characteristics like low birth weight and being difficult to control
- the child gives an account of the harm or danger they are in

Community-related:

- high crime rate
- lack of or few social services
- high poverty rate
- high unemployment rate (Craft (n.d.); Munro 2007; McGaw, Scully and Pritchard 2010)

### Risk factors for elder abuse

Caregivers:

- inability to cope with stress (lack of resilience)
- depression, which is common among caregivers
- lack of support from other potential caregivers
- the caregiver's perception that taking care of the elder is burdensome and without psychological reward
- substance abuse

Condition of the elder:

- the intensity of an elderly person's illness or dementia
- social isolation; i.e. the elder and caregiver are alone together almost all the time
- the elder's role, at an earlier time, as an abusive parent or spouse

- a history of domestic violence in the home
- the elder's own tendency towards verbal or physical aggression (Robinson, de Benedictis and Segal 2012)

*Risk factors for domestic violence*

- planning to leave or having recently left a relationship
- disputes over custody and access
- victims who are fearful for their life
- isolation from family and social supports
- pregnant (especially unplanned pregnancies)
- being stalked by partner or ex-partner
- in an overly controlling relationship
- being the victim of previous abuse (Dryden-Edwards and Stöppler (n.d.); Women's Aid 2006)

There is, however, no set of factors that absolutely differentiates the abusive from the non-abusive. As already discussed in relation to approaches to risk assessment above, professional judgement is needed in order to understand the potential relevance of risk factors in a given situation.

## Understanding Cause and Effect

The relevance of risk factors in a given situation should be understood by considering them in interaction rather than in isolation. Poverty is a risk factor shared across groups. Is this because there is a greater prevalence of abuse linked to the stress of poverty, or because families in poverty are more likely to come into contact with services, and therefore are more scrutinized and reported? It should be recognized that economic stress caused by poverty is widespread, but the majority of impoverished people do not pose a risk to their family members. Such stress is likely to be relevant in interaction with other factors, however; for example, poverty makes homelessness more likely and this increases the likelihood amongst the mentally ill of being a victim of violence. Individuals may in turn respond violently. Poverty may increase the impact of abuse on individuals. The impact of domestic violence on children is more complex than simply whether a child has witnessed or been subject to violence. For example, domestic violence may produce a reduction in parental warmth and well-being which may have a significant

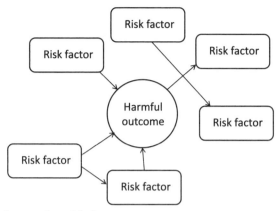

**Figure 2.1**  Interacting risk factors

impact on children's psychosocial development. Economic stress may add to the likelihood of a negative impact, for example, by reducing the ability of the non-abusive parent to seek solutions (Devaney 2008). Figure 2.1 captures this interactivity, illustrating how risk factors interact with each other to produce, directly or indirectly, a harmful outcome.

Professional judgements will take into account, therefore, not just the existence of a risk factor, but how that factor interacts with others and the patterns of causation that make a harmful outcome more likely. Estimations of risk still cannot be uncritically relied upon, however; assessors have to live with uncertainty and weigh up probability.

Judgements should also be based on assessments of strengths that may mitigate a risk. Figure 2.1 could be redrawn with the addition of strengths and protective factors, indicating how these interact with each other and with risk factors to make harmful outcomes less likely or to ameliorate impact.

## Activity 2.6  Risk Factors and Causation

Return to the risk factors for elder abuse above and consider this brief case example.

Mary and her elderly father have been referred because of some unexplained bruising on her father's arms. Mary says that she has gripped her father too tightly a couple of times, but that she was just trying to help him. He says she is sometimes rough with him but does not want to make a complaint. Mary describes her father as very difficult and demanding and never grateful. They live together in a small flat. Her mother is dead and her two siblings have no contact with them, apart from Christmas cards, having fallen out with their father after their mother's death. Mary has never married and has no children. She retired from work a year ago. Her father was a stern parent who used a great deal of physical chastisement and who was controlling towards Mary's mother. He is physically frail but still quick to argue and insists on his own way. Mary says that she is feeling depressed and has trouble sleeping and would like some tablets to help her feel better. It has all been much worse since she retired from part-time work and she is willing to engage with social work to help improve the situation.

In relation to this case, draw a diagram like that in Figure 2.1.

- Put in detail of the harmful outcome about which you are concerned; in this case physical and psychological harm to Mary's father.
- Put in specific examples of the risk factors that are relevant, using the list of risk factors for elder abuse as a starting point.
- Draw lines to summarize some of the key connections between risk factors and between individual factors and the harmful outcome.
- Now (use a different colour to make things clear) put in protective factors that serve to reduce risk.

You will have had no difficulty identifying many of the risk factors. If, however, you draw out lines of connection and causation, you may be helped to see more clearly possible implications for risk assessment. You are likely to think that Mary's depression is directly affecting the likelihood of abusive behaviour towards her father and could conclude that medication is an effective answer. However, as other risk factors are considered, you should see that social isolation is influencing her depression, as is her father's difficult behaviour. Both of these may be influenced by the lack of family contact. Her father's behaviour, while caused in large part by patterns set up throughout his life, may be worsened by a lack of contact with others and by living with Mary, who is depressed and uncommunicative. It is positive that Mary is willing to engage and that until recently work was a protective factor that helped ameliorate her isolation and depression.

Clearly, in a real case you would want much more information, but hopefully this has illustrated how thinking about causation and risk factors might make a difference. Helping Mary re-engage with her siblings might be a suitable intervention, for example. Until recently, she worked so she has skills and experiences that with some support can be drawn on to help her reduce her isolation. These interventions might sit alongside others, including those making sure that Mary and her father's well-being are monitored appropriately.

Ideally you should now repeat this with reference to a real case with which you are familiar, using the risk factors relevant to that case. Does this process make any difference to your assessment and analysis?

## *Thresholds*

Uncertainty in estimations of likelihood and impact is often worrying for practitioners because these judgements lead to decisions about thresholds: whether a risk is sufficient to trigger a particular intervention or service (Beckett 2008). In the case of Mary and her father above, judgements about the level of risk could have significant implications. Without the luxury of absolute certainty in social work this means that each risk decision will have the potential to lead to:

- a false positive where a risk is identified that does not in fact occur and where an unnecessary intervention has taken place; or
- a false negative where risk has wrongly been felt to be lower, an intervention is not provided and a serious harm does in fact take place.

False negatives are the outcomes that drive a lot of anxiety in professionals as they are more visible and easily identified and carry with them the fear of blame for the negative outcome (Beckett 2008). In situations where workers fear blame if serious outcomes occur, there is a temptation to adopt the precautionary principle and 'play safe' (Kemshall 1998a; Denney 2010). The impact of this on professional decision making will be considered further in subsequent chapters.

## A Range of Essential Skills and Abilities in Risk Assessment

In order to maximize the chances of balance and accuracy in risk assessment, but also in order to manage the demanding and emotionally tasking nature of the work, a practitioner will need skills and confidence in their ability to use those skills to achieve desired outcomes (Bandura 2007). Skills need to be used in an integrated way. All are relevant and have to work together; emphasizing favoured skills and not fully using others will be less effective. The skills considered in the remainder of this chapter are relevant across different areas of social work practice; however, the tailored application of general skills, together with specialist areas of knowledge, will be needed in individual practice settings. For example, working with children and families will require the understanding of child development mentioned earlier and an ability to communicate with children.

Skills for risk assessment include:

- organizational skills to plan the assessment process and to keep track of the sometimes complex processes of information gathering;
- the ability to communicate purposefully with service users, families and other professionals;
- skills in analysis which allow the assessor to see links, influences and patterns in the information being gathered;
- skills in making professional judgements based on evidence and on the meaning of that evidence;
- skills in recording both information and professional judgements;
- persistence in seeking information that is lacking;
- self-awareness and an ability to reflect on practice are also central. (Kemshall et al. 2011; Munro 2011)

---

### Activity 2.7   Self-Reflection: Strengths and Areas for Development

Use the approach suggested in the table below to reflect on your own areas of strength and ways in which you could improve your practice. This table could be used by experienced social workers identifying areas for professional development as part of appraisal. It could be used before a new job or at the start of a placement as part of your preparation.

| Abilities and skills | Areas of strength (note specific examples of strengths you are able to draw upon) | Areas for development (note specific examples of ways in which you need to develop your practice) |
|---|---|---|
| Organizational | | |

| Abilities and skills | Areas of strength (note specific examples of strengths you are able to draw upon) | Areas for development (note specific examples of ways in which you need to develop your practice) |
|---|---|---|
| Purposeful communication | | |
| Analysis | | |
| Professional judgement | | |
| Recording | | |
| Persistence | | |
| Self-awareness and reflection | | |

The chapter goes on to consider these areas in more detail. You are asked to return to your reflection once you have read the rest of the chapter.

## Organizational Skills

Preparation was included in Figure 1.1 as an essential stage of the risk-assessment and management process. A worker should think about the range of information likely to be needed, and from whom, and plan accordingly. In doing so deadlines, timescales, practicalities and resources should be taken into account. Sometimes poor practice can result from seemingly trivial issues, for example a missed home visit because a worker hasn't planned ahead and arranged for a colleague to accompany them.

Once the risk-assessment process is under way, organizational skills remain essential to ensure, for example, that all necessary sources of information have been followed up and that relevant individuals are kept informed about the progress of the assessment. A systematic approach to assessment needs skilful time management, including:

- prioritizing and sequencing activities;
- organizing and recording data;

- reliability; and
- attention to detail. (Trevithick 2000; Parker and Bradley 2007)

These skills are equally relevant for risk management. The following activity (adapted from Baker, Kelly and Wilkinson 2011: 144) requires consideration of all of the elements of planning that underpin an organized approach to assessment practice.

---

**Activity 2.8   Planning an Assessment**

Use the list below to improve planning for a piece of assessment practice. This would be useful for new practitioners and students and also for experienced staff to review planning in a case that has not gone as expected.

- Plan for any deadlines, taking account of other work commitments that might get in the way.
- What information do you need to gather from whom – where and how? How much time will this be likely to take?
- What home visits will be needed? Is there interviewing space available for office interviews?
- Plan ahead for difficult-to-obtain information, for example from a busy professional.
- Are there issues relating to the characteristics or context of the service user to take into account, for example needing more than one contact for a service user who is likely to find the interview process stressful, or difficult to understand?
- Will you need additional help, e.g. the services of an interpreter, specialist assessments, or consultation with colleagues and managers? Leave enough time for them to do their jobs.
- Allocate sufficient time for recording, report writing and for sharing the results of your assessment with its subject and with other key individuals.

---

## Communication with Other Professionals

Communication is at the heart of risk-assessment practice. In order to gather together the information needed to make judgements about risk, workers need to be able to obtain and make sense of information from a range of sources. This communication can make a real difference to outcomes: for example, good communication about long-term care for an older person can make an unnecessary move without a proper consideration of alternatives less likely. Multi-agency communication needs to operate in a way that does not exclude the subject of the assessment, with the perspectives of the older person, for example, also remaining at the heart of decision making (McDonald 2010b).

For effective communication to take place, there needs to be clarity about roles and responsibilities and an understanding of the importance of sharing information on a need-to-know basis (Barker and Hodes 2007). Communication is shaped by legislation including the Data Protection Act 1998, the Human Rights Act 1998 and Article 8 of the European Convention of Human Rights. Practitioners need to follow guidance for their role and setting in order to balance the protection of an individual's right to privacy and the need to share information to prevent harm (DCSF 2008). Ideally, that communication will take place with consent, but this is not always possible. 'The usual rules do not apply when you are concerned that a child is suffering, or at risk of suffering, significant harm' (Munro 2007: 34).

In child protection, practitioners encounter 'complex interactions that require not only skill, but also appreciation of issues relating to power or status, and a degree of confidence in one's own professional worth' (Keys 2009b: 326). Practitioners therefore have to be self-conscious about their communication with others, sure of the knowledge and skill they can draw on, but respectful of the knowledge and skills of others. Edwards et al. (2009: 61) talk about being 'professionally multilingual', that is, knowing enough about the work of others and their professional language to be able to communicate effectively and to respect the work that they do. Practitioners need to be able to:

- articulate the evidence and knowledge base for their practice decisions (Osmond and O'Connor 2004);
- integrate and communicate knowledge about their area of practice, for example, bringing together knowledge about child development and knowledge about a particular individual and family;
- be professionally confident enough to draw on the knowledge of others. (Nash 2010)

As well as a good understanding of theory and research evidence and of the individuals and families with whom they are working, social work practitioners need to understand the process of communication itself. It is not straightforward. Reder and Duncan (2004a) draw attention to the importance of practitioners understanding that, when they communicate to other professionals, they communicate both facts and the meanings that they have attributed to those facts. For example, factual information about the regularity of contact of an older person with family members might be communicated in a way that suggests that the family doesn't care, or in a way that suggests that the family has practical difficulties but wants to be involved. Subtle differences in tone and choice of language might have a significant impact on decisions made about how to involve family members in ongoing decision making. In an analysis of reviews of child deaths and serious injuries, Brandon, Dodsworth and Rumball (2005) make the point that what is most helpful to share is information not just about symptoms, but also about their impact on the behaviour of family members and others. This means that it is important not just to share risk factors but to share understanding of their interaction and effect as suggested in Figure 2.1. Someone may abuse alcohol but what impact does that abuse have on their behaviour towards the children concerned? Is that impact direct or indirect?

In conducting a risk assessment, assessors need to understand their own communications with others and the messages they may be giving, as well as understanding the influences affecting others' communications with them. Guidance on multi-agency participation in the children's workforce emphasizes communication skills such as providing 'timely, appropriate, succinct information' and being 'able to use clear language to communicate information unambiguously' (CWDC: 18:21).

The most well-known model of communication uses the analogy of transmitting information from a source to a receiver (Donnelly and Neville 2008). An instance of communication will include the content of the message, but also the processes and methods used and an understanding of who is receiving the message and how they are hearing it. Donnelly and Neville expand this idea to explain that communication is usually not a one-off process but something that develops over time between the transmitter and receiver. The process of communication over time can be disrupted by a range of influences. Physical (noisy office, pressure of time) and psychological (anxiety about the decisions that need to be made) pressures and confusion between transmitter and receiver about how language and concepts are being used can all make a difference.

---

**Activity 2.9  Communication**

Choose a situation where communication played an important role in assessment. Answer the following questions from the point of view of both the transmitter and the receiver of that information. Were there any differences in perspective between the two?

- Who needed the information and why?
- What did they need to know and when – how urgently?
- Where was the information received?
- How did the transmitter want the receiver to use the information? (Adapted from Baker, Kelly and Wilkinson 2011)

If there were different perspectives, what in your opinion caused those differences? For example, were they influenced by pressures of time and/ or the physical environment and/or by differences in understanding about the meanings of key terms?

---

## Communicating with Service Users

Much of the information that is needed to conduct a risk assessment is held by the individuals most closely concerned – the child, the mentally ill person, or the older person who is the subject of the assessment and those people, including family members, closest to them. Engaging in effective communication with those individuals is also a skilled process, even more so bearing in mind the complex balances discussed earlier in this chapter. Power differentials in assessment relationships need to be borne in mind. Social workers should be sensitive to differences in power and able to manage those differences skilfully (Milner and O'Byrne 2009). Koprowska (2010) highlights the skills needed to communicate effectively with a range of service users who have particular communication needs, including minority languages, deafness and learning disabilities. For such service users and for children, power issues may be even more acute but practitioners should not make assumptions about any service user and should exercise skills such as active listening and adopting clear, specific and unambiguous language.

Power can be exercised in subtle and complex ways. Munro (2011) found that in general practitioners had difficulty in communicating effectively with male service users. This may be a result of some male subjects of risk assessments exercising their own limited power through their conduct in interview to attempt to control or influence the process. On the other hand, assessors are likely to interpret denial of responsibility or a refusal to discuss abuse as a failure to take responsibility and therefore as evidence of increased risk. While this may be the case, there is not an inevitable connection between the two. Denial might be indicative of shame or an acceptance that abusive behaviour is socially disapproved of and this recognition may help support avoidance of such behaviour in the future (Maruna and Mann 2006). Judgements about the meaning of behaviours are constantly being made and need to be reflected on by open-minded practitioners to ensure that they don't distort communication and that they retain the ability to listen effectively to the service user.

Communication with service users is important for the process as a whole. We lack a robust evidence base for the skills that are needed but do have some important pointers to an essential skill base (Keys 2009a). In order to achieve a cooperative relationship with a parent, important skills include: listening skills; demonstrating respect; setting clear boundaries; and role clarification. Trotter (2002), in one of the few studies to have included outcome measures, also identifies the importance of role clarification and in addition cites collaborative problem-solving skills, pro-social and relationship skills, empathy and optimism and the reinforcement of positives, while not minimizing concerns about harm. His study found that when these skills were used, there were better outcomes.

Forrester et al. (2008a), using role-played scenarios with abusive parents, investigated the skills that child protection workers actually used in interview and found that they tended to use closed questions and rarely reflected back or identified positives. Empathic social workers who used more open and positive approaches created less resistance and gained more disclosure from simulated clients while retaining role clarity and raising concerns appropriately. These findings are echoed by Ferguson (2010) who talks about the need to pay detailed attention to practitioner behaviour during home visits, and how to make use of the physical opportunities for contact and observation.

Munro (2011) found evidence that practitioners are under-confident about communicating with children and suggests that more training would be helpful. In the context of obtaining information about potential abuse from children, great care should be exercised and assessors should be very alert to the dangers of putting words into children's mouths or misunderstanding their responses. The kinds of questions used are important, for example using the active rather than the passive voice:

- Was mummy hit by the man?
- Did the man hit mummy? (Koprowska 2010: 104)

The latter question is less likely to be misunderstood. The same author also suggests that leading or over-complex questions should be avoided, as should questions that use the negative form. In a study of investigative interviews with children, Evans et al. (2010) found that when the interviewer paraphrased and repeated inaccurately back to a child, the child was unlikely to correct any errors. The power in the relationship again may distort the child's behaviour. Of course, in order to exercise these skills appropriately, social workers have to understand their importance and the centrality of listening to the child and other vulnerable individuals as part of risk assessment. Brandon et al. (2008a: 324) found that 'Where the needs of the parents overshadowed those of the children, the professional engagement was with the parents and children were missed.' This was found to be particularly the case when children were pre-verbal, suggesting that, as well as skills in communication, workers need sufficient knowledge to judge non-verbal behaviour and other worrying signs with accuracy.

---

**Activity 2.10   Observing and Analysing Practice**

Arguably the most effective way of developing your own skills is to be observed and to receive feedback on your interactions with service users. All risk assessors should occasionally have interviews with service users recorded or observed and should receive feedback from a skilled observer on the quality of their interactions. The following checklist may provide a simple but useful guide for that observer who should give specific examples to illustrate their feedback.

- Were both open and closed questions used appropriately and what was the balance between them?
- Were questions framed appropriately for the interviewee, using understandable language and, where necessary, the active voice?
- Were skills in summarizing and reflecting back used effectively and accurately?

- Were positives identified and reflected back to the interviewee?
- Were difficult subjects discussed clearly and openly, without unnecessary confrontation?
- Did the interviewer model optimism for the future?

While these exact questions may not be appropriate for all service users, gathering and understanding feedback about service users' experience of the interaction is also valuable.

Smale and Tuson (1993) identified three models of interaction with service users: questioning, administrative and exchange. The first two are based on expert knowledge. In the first, the interviewer sets the agenda; in the second, the agency provides the structure for the interview. The last approach assumes that service users are the experts in their own problems and is a more equal exchange. In much risk-assessment practice, workers are increasingly guided by processes and tools that are intended to ensure that they pay attention to all relevant concerns. These approaches fit within the questioning and administrative templates and have their strengths; supporting consistency for example. The danger is that over-relying on a highly structured approach may cause interviewers to lose sight of the impact of relationships in the assessment process. Agency-centred assessments may, for example, make it more likely that the efforts of older people to understand and communicate their situation in a narrative way – that is, by telling their story – are overlooked (Richards 2000). Driscoll (2009) talks about the importance of restoring a child-centred approach in child protection. Again, a balance is needed; skilful workers should be able to be clear and consistent about their role, while using empathic skills, to enable service users to share in the process of defining the problem and seeking potential solutions.

### Activity 2.11   Reflecting on an Interview

This activity takes place following a risk-assessment interview. It could be used, for example, as part of supervision or to review a recorded interview as part of a training package.

Use the following questions to reflect on an interview, making a note not just of your views but of the evidence within the interview that supports your judgements.

- What balance was achieved between role clarity and empathy with the interviewee?
- Was the interviewer able to balance structured information gathering with developing a relationship with the other person?

If more than one person has observed the interview, it would be useful to compare notes.

Alternatively, if you were reflecting on an interview of your own, you could use these questions to guide a structured discussion about the interview with a colleague or supervisor.

## Analysis judgement and recording

Practitioners should be able not just to gather information but also to understand its significance. They need to make decisions about what information to seek out and about the significance and impact of specific pieces of information on their risk assessment and eventual risk-management plans. Chapter 3 goes into a great deal more detail about decision making and judgement. For now, it is enough to remind ourselves that understandings of both the general – for example, patterns of behaviour in a particular client group – and the individual – how one member of that group experiences the world and responds – will equip risk assessors to weigh up historical, personal and environmental information and enable them to make informed judgements about risk. 'A more person-centred approach to risk and dementia concentrates upon identifying risky situations for individuals with dementia rather than viewing every person with dementia as being at equal risk' (Manthorpe and Moriarty 2010: 9). The risk assessor has to understand the individual in order to both personalize the assessment and work out how general risk factors apply in a particular set of circumstances to a particular individual.

### Activity 2.12    The Quality of Information

The following questions help you think through the quality of information received in a particular case. You could use it to review a case you currently have or recently worked on where information you received made a significant difference. If you were a supervisor, you could use it as part of consultation with a member of staff or student about a difficult decision based on particular received information. Is the meaning of this information clear?

- What is the reliability of the source?
- What does this information tell us about the pattern of behaviour and about the triggers and circumstances leading to risk?
- Is there any evidence of a changing pattern of risky behaviours?

Do the answers suggest any specific action?

Information gathered and understood has to be recorded and recording systems can feel unhelpful, over-cumbersome, for example, and too demanding of time. Careful attention must be paid to recording, however (Baker, Kelly and Wilkinson 2011). Recorded information provides one of the most important ways in which defensible practice can be evidenced. If used well, it is an aid to analysis and a way of checking the substance and validity of evidence. Recording is also a key form of communication with others during ongoing work with a service user. It may have a significant impact. Information recorded in assessment tools and case records can continue to influence perceptions and decision making over time (O'Rourke 2010).

### Individual attributes and reflection

In developing practice for the better, attention should focus not just on skills but on the individual attributes that help practitioners use those skills effectively. 'The literature has suggested that self-awareness, reflexivity and a willingness to change one's mind may be essential qualities,' while 'persistence and the confidence to challenge others may ultimately be as important for the child's welfare as any skill' (Keys 2009b: 329). In the same paper, she suggests that managing the emotional impact of such work, while not usually identified as a skill, should also be addressed. Practitioners working with families where there are concerns about abuse or neglect are often faced with a lack of cooperation which might include missed appointments, partial or ambivalent compliance, keeping some information from social workers and, at the extreme, hostility and threats of violence

(Brandon et al. 2008a). Darlington, Healy and Feeney (2010) found that to engage parents in participative decision making, where there may be conflict between participation and child protection, required the use of relationship skills but that these were given too little attention in practice. Managing conflict requires an ability to manage the worker's own feelings. The emotional impact of practice is discussed further in chapter 7.

---

**Activity 2.13  Returning to Your Attributes and Skills**

Earlier in the chapter, you were asked to complete a table about your attributes and skills, strengths and areas for development. Return to that now. Would you add anything else as a result of reading this chapter?

---

## Conclusion

This chapter looks at the skilful nature of risk assessment, the place of assessment tools alongside the centrality of professional judgement and of knowledge skills and characteristics of risk assessors. Risk assessment requires a balance of competing demands drawing on a range of information and knowledge. For example, estimations of future risk are necessarily uncertain and should be based on, but not limited by, risk factors identified by research. Patterns of causation and the effect of strengths and resilience should also be part of the assessment; risk taking as well as risk avoidance is part of the professional task. Risk assessment should be purposeful and lead to informed decision making and subsequent risk management. Chapters that follow will explore those components in more depth.

FURTHER READING

Beckett, C. (2008) 'Risk uncertainty and thresholds', in M. Calder (ed.), *Contemporary Risk Assessment in Safeguarding Children*. Lyme Regis: Russell House, pp. 40–51. For a clear and helpful explanation of risk assessment and thresholds.
Carr, S. (2010) *Enabling Risk: Securing Safety: Self-directed Support and Personal Budgets*. London: SCIE. Specifically concerned with personal

budgets but uses this to explore the balance between managing potential harm and allowing for appropriate risk taking.

There are also very helpful books exploring practice with specific service users that help to contextualize risk. They include:

Baker, K., Kelly, G. and Wilkinson, B. (2011) *Assessment in Youth Justice.* Bristol: Policy Press.
McDonald, A. (2010) *Social Work with Older People.* Cambridge: Polity.
Munro, E. (2008) *Effective Child Protection*, 2nd edn. London: Sage.

# 3

# *The Art of Decision Making*

Risk work requires 'good judgement', i.e. judgement which is well informed, balanced, reasoned and critical, avoiding bias and discrimination. The problem is that 'good judgement' cannot be guaranteed, and the human minds exercising such judgement do not do so within a vacuum. Social work is characterized by the need to make judgements, to make decisions, about almost everything at almost every moment of the day. Some decisions are routine, even second nature to us. Others we perceive as more problematic and challenging. In truth, both types can get us into trouble where risk is concerned. The routinization of risk decisions, for example, has resulted in child protection failures (Corby 2000) by reducing alertness to changes in circumstances and diminishing responsiveness to escalating risk (Munro 1995). Literally, we do not see what we are not looking for, and routine tasks tend to erode vigilance. Visits are made to meet the requirements of making a visit, but within a busy working schedule practitioners might not adopt an 'investigative stance' in their contacts with service users. That is, where routinization is combined with bureaucracy, risk assessment becomes embedded in administrative tasks like completing forms, inputting computer data, or routinely completing tick-box risk assessments, critical and reflective decision making can be further eroded (Munro 2010a, b; Peckover et al. 2011). In such situations, when investigated with the benefit of hindsight, practitioners can appear to have been unresponsive to risk, but in essence routinization has resulted in the atrophy of vigilance both in the risk system and in individual risk practice (Kemshall 1998b, 2003; Reason 1997, 2009). However, in the busy world of work, routinization is inevitable. It is how practitioners cope with high caseloads, and it is how busy managers administer agency systems and processes. It contains the seeds of risk failure but is very difficult to avoid.

Problematic and challenging decisions about risk are more easily recognized, but also present difficulties for practitioners. Such decisions can make us uncomfortable, resulting in 'risk avoidance', with decisions delayed and action drifting until we are literally forced to act. Such actions can be unreflective, inappropriate, rushed and unhelpful. In such situations practitioners can feel under pressure, feeling that they are 'catching up' with events and that they have lost control of the case. Stress and emotion begin to take the place of reason and critical reflection. Challenging decisions can also make us defensive, fearful that we will make a mistake and acutely aware of public and media scrutiny. In these situations, the 'precautionary principle' (COMEST 2005) can take over. In brief, we take the view that absence of evidence of risk does not mean no risk, and we tend to overestimate both the likelihood of risk and the extent of its impact (Slovic 2000). We are 'precautionary' in our decision making. This can result in over-intrusive responses, with negative consequences for service users and the potential waste of resources. Risk avoidance can result in practitioners being unresponsive to risk, and risk precaution can result in over-intrusion. This can result in false positives and false negatives as outlined in chapter 2.

The pitfalls are many, so how can they be avoided? Attention to three key areas can help practitioners to improve their decision making. These are:

1   the skills required to exercise sound judgement and make good decisions about risk;
2   understanding the emotions, values, attitudes and biases that affect decision making in negative ways;
3   alternative frameworks for decision making, for example rehearsing risk scenarios.

These will now be discussed in turn.

## Skills Required to Exercise Sound Judgement and Make Good Decisions About Risk

As we have seen, good decision making does not come naturally and there are numerous barriers to sound judgement. Decision making is an 'art' that can be learnt and improved. Critical to good decision making are the skills of *analysis* and *critical reasoning*. Analytical skills are important to assess the vast amount of information and data received daily by practitioners. *What does this mean?* is perhaps the most critical question we can ask of information we receive. The second is perhaps *what should I now do in the light of this information?* Each of these areas will be considered in turn. The first in essence concerns *judgement*, that is, 'the ways in which people integrate multiple, probabilistic, potentially conflicting cues to arrive at an understanding of the situation'; and the second concerns *decision making*, that is, how 'people choose what to do next in the face of uncertain consequences and conflicting goals' (Goldstein and Hogarth 1997: 4). Sound judgement depends on how we receive, interrogate and use information. Making a good decision depends on how well we recognize and manage uncertainty and deal with the potential for differing and at times competing outcomes.

*Exercising sound judgement: critically appraising information*

It is what is done with information, rather than its simple accumulation, that leads to more analytic assessments and safer practice (Brandon et al. 2008a: 3).

Some key questions for the risk assessor to ask are:

- What does this information mean?
- What is the reliability of the source of this information?
- What does this information tell me about the pattern of behaviour?
- What does this information tell me about the triggers and circumstances leading to risk?
- Is there any evidence of an escalating pattern of risky behaviours?

Information is always filtered and subject to interpretation against the background of our existing knowledge, values, bias and stereotypes (Moore 1996). Meaning is attributed, rather than coming to us in pure form. For example, Munro has shown how information about parenting is heavily framed by the initial views that practitioners form of parents, and is rarely subject to review, despite further negative information (1999, 2008a). Information can also be ambiguous, deriving meaning from the context, circumstances and previous history. Consider the following case example:

---

### Case illustration: release from youth custody

A young man is about to be released from Youth Custody. He states his home address as his release address.

**Commentary**
This home address can be *either* a resilience factor, providing support, stability and protection, *or* a risk factor, taking the young man back into an offending and antisocial network with numerous pressures to reoffend.

Whether the home address is considered a resilience or a risk factor depends upon:

* knowledge of the family, including history of offending, parental control and any family triggers or stressors that have contributed to his offending in the past; or knowledge of the family as a source of protective factors, stability and support;
* the particular circumstances in which the young man has offended in the past, for example with family members, in response to family stressors (i.e. arguments), and so on; or only outside the family and whether pro-social support can be expected from the family;
* proximity of the family home to the young man's local peer group and offending network.

Without such detailed knowledge, a proper assessment of the home address as either a resilience or a risk factor cannot be made.

---

Now consider the following activity:

---

### Activity 3.1   Considering Ambiguous Factors

This exercise can be done using a current case from your workload, a case from a student placement, or a case study provided to students by your social work course tutor.

Take a current or recent case where there were ambiguous factors, that is, factors that might indicate protection, a source of strength or support for the individual; but which could also function as risk factors, that is, indicative of risk in the situation.

List them, and make a note of whether the factors were interpreted as resilience or as risk. What was the basis for each decision?

---

You will have realized that it is important to place information in its context in order to fully understand what it means, and that the source of information can impact on its reliability. Such reliability is of course critical to sound risk assessment. For example, police officers managing sex offenders in the community would rank information from a police or probation officer about a directly observed behaviour, for example, a sex offender outside a school, as a 'class one' information source, fully reliable and evidenced. On the other hand, the self-report of a sex offender about their own behaviour, for example, about their daily whereabouts, is 'class four', that is non-observed, not evidenced, and not corroborated. This is not to say that sex offender self-reports cannot be truthful, but it does indicate that they need to be tested, for example by another source. Grading sources in this way is an interesting exercise and can assist practitioners in weighing information, especially information that is sometimes conflicting and contrary. For example, grading the source, reliability and usefulness of information might have assisted decision making in recent UK child protection failures where over-reliance on parents/guardians/carers as a source of information on child well-being was a serious failure (for example, Victoria Climbié and Baby Peter; Laming 2003, 2009 respectively). The following activity provides a helpful test on information sources:

---

**Activity 3.2   Testing Information Sources**

This exercise can be done using a current case from your workload, a case from a student placement, or a case study provided to students by your social work course tutor.

Take a case you are currently working on.

1   List all the information that comes from a class one source: that is, it is directly observed, well-evidenced and is corroborated.
2   List all the information that comes from a class four source: that is, it is based on client/user self-report, is not well-evidenced and cannot be corroborated by any other source.
3   What does the relative balance between your answers to 1 and 2 tell you about the quality of information that you are about to base your risk assessment on?
4   What action will you now take and why?

Class one sources are critical to sound judgements of risk, but social workers are often in the position of making decisions quickly without the benefit of full information. The balance between our information sources isn't always ideal. You may be surprised to learn how much information that we use in assessments actually comes from class four sources, that is, it is often uncorroborated and lacking in an evidence base.

Information from clients and service users can of course be reliable and there are instances where they are the best assessors of their own situation. For example, direct payments are predicated on the idea that service users best know what they need and should be enabled to purchase it directly (Littlechild and Glasby 2011). However, it is critical that practitioners can distinguish when clients and service users are likely to be a good source of risk information and when they are not. To make such a distinction, it is helpful to ask:

- What are the likely motivations for the service user in expressing this view?
- What evidence and experience is the service user's view likely to be rooted in, and how robust is this evidence and experience?
- What is the service user trying to achieve from you by giving you this information?

A clear understanding of service-user motivations and the basis for the risk information they provide helps practitioners to evaluate what they are being told and why they are being told it. Putting it bluntly, parents potentially engaged in child abuse will have very different motivations for information disclosure than persons seeking access to direct payments. Service users can also be members of larger family or social networks, and information from different sources within such networks can conflict. Consider the following case study:

---

### Case study: Freda

Freda is a 77-year-old white woman living alone in council accommodation. Her family have noticed that she is becoming increasingly forgetful, and that the household tasks she previously managed are increasingly difficult for her. Her son recently visited and found a gas ring on and a saucepan boiled dry. Neighbours have complained about the smell of gas. Freda has always been fiercely independent and resents any reliance upon family or 'interfering social workers'. She insists that she is managing quite well and does not require any assistance. However, her family remain worried and, after monitoring the situation for some weeks, feel they must refer her to the local social services department.

- How can each of these differing views be tested or corroborated?
- What would count as an independent view of risk in this case?
- How would you reconcile the differing views of Freda and her extended family?

(Reproduced with permission from Kemshall 2002a)

This is a relatively common situation but is nonetheless challenging. To test and corroborate what is happening in this situation, the social worker might consider observing Freda or carrying out a more extensive assessment of Freda's day-to-day functioning. This would require negotiation with Freda, who is possibly fearful of losing her home and moving into residential care. The social worker may need to allay these fears, and an assessment may, for example, indicate how Freda can remain at home with care and support. In this case, establishing the range of possible desirable outcomes especially for Freda will be critical to gaining cooperation from all parties. An 'independent' view of risk may not be entirely possible, but the social worker can seek other sources (e.g. from Freda's GP), observation, and face-to-face discussion with Freda in order to establish as balanced and evidenced a picture of risk as possible. The social worker also does not need to adopt and start from the family's perspective that Freda cannot remain at home. Rather, the assessment can start from the position of what can be done to mitigate the risks presented by Freda staying at home – this may generate an acceptable option for all parties, with the overriding outcome being Freda's safety.

Practitioners also have to evaluate what the information means, in effect what it can tell them about patterns of behaviour, the triggers and circumstances leading to risk, and any evidence of an escalating pattern of risky behaviours. Such an evaluation can only take place against the background of adequate knowledge about risk factors, risky behaviours and the factors that lead to escalation in particular situations and circumstances. Such knowledge cannot be taken for granted. Consider the following questions:

1 What are the main predictors of child physical abuse? List at least five.

2  What are the main predictors of violence in mentally disordered persons? List between two and five predictors.
3  What are the main risk factors for elder abuse?
4  What are the main risk factors for domestic violence?

(These risk factors were presented in chapter 2. If you cannot recall
them, go back and check them now.)

If the area asked about is your area of expertise, then you should
be able to list the correct answers quickly and use these predictors in
your assessment of individual cases – for example, to identify domestic violence. If none of the areas is within your area of expertise,
consider a similar question about the main predictors of risk for your
area of work. The key point is that you should have sufficient up-to-
date knowledge to list them accurately. If you do not, then your
assessments are already flawed as, despite large amounts of information coming your way, you do not have the basic knowledge to
identify relevant risk factors or to see patterns of risky behaviour
developing over time (Baker 2007). Patterns can only be recognized
accurately against a sound knowledge base (Baker 2007; Schwalbe
2008).

### Exercising sound judgement: weighing up the evidence

Practitioners are also required to weigh up competing, sometimes
conflicting, information and to distinguish between the reliability of
different information sources. However, we prefer certainty and tend
to rationalize doubts away (Lehrer 2009). We go with our initial
preferred option, the first view that we formed, and we are reluctant
to change our minds, even in the face of new information to the
contrary. Munro (1995) has called this 'the power of first impression',
and this initial appraisal of the person or situation influences all our
future decisions about them. This 'first impression bias' has had a
negative impact on child protection. For example, it was identified
as long ago as 1975 in the inquiry into the death of John George
Aukland (Department of Health and Social Security 1975; Reder,
Duncan and Gray 1993). According to Munro, the Aukland report
showed how 'social workers uncritically accepted false information
from the husband who made a good impression on them while dis-
believing the wife who presented herself less favourably' (1995: 59).
This search for certainty and the failure to revise first impressions has
played its role in subsequent child protection tragedies ranging from
Jasmine Beckford (London Borough of Brent 1985) to Victoria

Climbié (Laming 2003) and Baby Peter (Laming 2009; see also Reder, Duncan and Gray 1993 for a review of a number of relevant cases).

Far from exercising critical reasoning, we opt for the 'first impression or certainty bias', particularly in conditions of pressure, uncertainty and challenge (Kahneman, Slovic and Tversky 1990; see Carson and Bain 2008 on health and social work risks). Hollows has described this as a natural reaction to a 'flood of data', particularly where information is contradictory (2008: 56). Cognitive shortcuts enable us to navigate the complexity of the world and to manage competing demands (Strachan and Tallant 1997) and can literally 'anchor' us to the world so that all our subsequent views and decisions are 'anchored' to this initial view (Carson and Bain 2008: 194). In situations of stress, anxiety and blame, the 'certainty bias' is very powerful (Smith, McMahon and Nursten 2003).

To combat this, practitioners and their managers need to critically reflect on whether they are falling into the 'certainty trap' and adopt a questioning and interrogative stance towards information and data and to information sources. Critical reasoning is also important. This requires openness to contrary viewpoints and arguments. Decision making can become complacent and routine; it is therefore important to test decisions against what the evidence actually says. Munro (1995) argues that the bias of first impression needs to be actively challenged by practitioners and their managers by adopting the following steps:

- making the first impression and the evidence it is based on explicit;
- explicitly checking any first impression against contrary or disconfirming views/perspectives/evidence;
- making a deliberate and conscious effort to think of evidence for the opposing view.

This may mean paying attention to the information that most challenges your deeply held beliefs about the situation or the case, and listening to the things you most want to dismiss (Lehrer 2009). Some key questions for risk assessors to ask are:

- Does this information disconfirm what I already believe?
- Why does this information make me uncomfortable? Why am I tempted to discount it?
- What other consequences or possible outcomes does this information require me to consider?

- What changes to my risk-assessment and my risk-management plan does this information require me to make?

### *Making good decisions about risk: developing critical reasoning and reflection*

Practitioners intuitively simplify complex judgements (Munro 1999), a contention supported not only by Munro's own investigations of social work practice but by a large body of psychological research (see e.g. Slovic 2000 for a full review). This is reflected in how practitioners seek and use information and evidence. As numerous child protection inquiries have shown, practitioners rarely meet the gold standard of analytic reasoning rooted in a 'step-by-step, conscious, logically defensible process' (Hammond 1996: 60; Munro 1999).

---

**Activity 3.3   Case Study Exercise**

This exercise can be done using a current case from your workload, a case from a student placement, or a case study provided to students by your social work course tutor.

Read the case study and then consider the questions. Make a note of your answers as you will need them later when considering the feedback.

**Case study of Jody and family**
Jody, aged 23, is the mother of three children: Liam, aged five, Tommy, aged three, and Cheryl, aged 18 months. Her partner Joe, father to the two youngest children, has recently completed an 18-month prison sentence for drug-related offences and assault and has returned to live in the family home. They live in privately rented accommodation in an area with few amenities and high levels of poverty and unemployment. Neither is employed and they rely upon state benefits.

Jody has been known to social work services since she was nine when she first came into care as a victim of physical abuse resulting from her mother's alcohol misuse and mental ill health. She experienced a number of periods with different foster carers and attempted returns to her family until, at age 14, she disclosed that her mother's partner had been sexually abusing her. Although no criminal charges were made, the decision was taken to remove Jody to a children's unit. Her behaviour was seen as challenging and difficult to manage but she stayed there until obtaining her own tenancy at age 17. At that point Jody was pregnant and she continued to accept support from social work services. Jody had no contact with her family as a result of the allegations of abuse and she very much welcomed the support of the social worker, nursery staff and health visitor during Liam's early years. Liam was seen as a healthy child who was meeting milestones and, although Jody was quite isolated and lonely, she was assessed as being responsive and alert to Liam's needs. Support to the family ended when Jody left the area to move in with Joe.

Contact with health services began again following the birth of Tommy and the health visitor referred the family to social work services, expressing concerns about Jody being depressed and the general physical care of the home and both children. A nursery place was found for Liam and social workers were involved for a short time, their main focus being to work alongside Jody to link her and the children into local services. Following the birth of Cheryl, and during Joe's prison sentence, a child protection investigation was done as both boys were left alone in the home when Jody had taken Cheryl to a GP appointment and failed to return home until some time later. Another investigation took place following an incident of domestic abuse involving Joe and Jody, shortly after Joe was released from prison. At this time, concerns were again noted about the physical care of the children and the poor conditions of the home. The three children are now subject to supervision requirements. All agencies working with Jody and Joe have noted a new resistance to engaging with services since Joe has returned to the family home. The health visitor has noted increased visits to the GP and Accident and Emergency department in relation to Cheryl who is quite a sickly child and who suffers from asthma. Her contact with the family has been less frequent of late. Contact with social workers seems to be initiated by Jody asking for financial assistance but practitioners are finding the family harder to contact and engage with. None of the three children are attending nursery regularly but, when they do attend, the two boys in particular are said to respond well to staff and activities. Cheryl is seen as a clingy and withdrawn child who prefers to be near to staff rather than with the other children.

(Kindly provided by Anne Ritchie, Dept of Social Work, University of the West of Scotland)

Questions:

1  What assumptions have you made about the case?
2  What information have you given the most weight to and why?
3  What do you think the problem might be?

The case study exercise helps to demonstrate how difficult it is to follow the step-by-step logical process of reasoning advocated by Hammond, particularly where information is missing and we are required to formulate a view quickly; and how easy it is to fill in the gaps with assumptions, speculations and problem-solving (Kida 2006; Schacter 2001; Tavris and Aaronson 2007). It is also easier to be drawn to evidence and information presented, particularly where it is vivid and concrete, rather than to suspend belief and proactively search for what we don't know (Munro 1995, 1996, 1999; Slovic 2000; Prins 2005). The tendency for intuitive reasoning to predominate in social work practice has been much documented (see Munro 1998, 1999 for examples), and also much critiqued for its over-reliance on bias and heuristics (see Schwalbe 2004 for a review). Heuristics are in effect the 'rules of thumb' or shortcuts in thinking which we all use to assess situations, including situations of risk (Gilovich, Griffin and Kahneman 2002; Kahneman, Slovic and Tversky 1990). Heuristics are essentially devices that enable us to frame our knowledge and interpretations of the world (Denney 2005). Such framing helps us to deal with information overload and to make sense out of disorder and chaos. Consequently, heuristics can result in subjective perceptions of risk that are significantly different to the objective probability of the risk actually occurring. Crime risks are a case in point, where media coverage can heighten subjective perceptions of risk beyond the rates of crime supported by current available evidence (Kemshall 1997b: 249, 256; see also Roberts and Hough 2005). In social work practice, it can result in risk assessments that are not sufficiently rooted in the evidence. Now consider the case study of Jody and her family again.

---

### Activity 3.4   Case Study Exercise and Reflection

- What do you think are the risk factors in this situation?
- How likely are they to occur and in what timescale?
- What would be the impact of them occurring and to whom?

Make a record of your answers.

(Kindly supplied by Anne Ritchie, Department of Social Work, University of the West of Scotland)

---

This may have felt like a more informed and precise assessment. However, it is important to again consider how limited this assessment may be.

---

### Case Study: Activity 3.4 Feedback

Using this approach to the assessment of risk is likely to leave you with a limited picture of this family, their needs and apparent risks that may deny their strengths and the possible benefits of living with and managing risk. There are clearly a wide range of acute risks but the social worker should also be assessing those risks whose impact may have longer-term consequences upon the well-being of the family. The environment and the family's social circumstances need also to be assessed for the risks they present to all family members. The risks should be weighed against the potential losses and benefits associated with each possible risk factor, and social workers should always strive to encourage service users to make informed choices about whether or not they wish to take risks. This might not always be possible, particularly when we are working with compulsory measures of care and protection.

The avoidance of risk at all costs is very likely to lead us into a minefield beset with new dangers so the social worker's job is to weigh all risks against possible losses and benefits. The social worker should offer a critical evaluation of the assessment and interventions, considering possible bias, consequences and outcomes of each course of action. Common errors in the assessment of risk primarily centre on how we understand the notion of probability. Risk-assessment tools are often used in our search for certainty without a critical overview of their limitations and inherent bias. Critical practitioners are required to make informed decisions about *unique* circumstances and about the probability of events happening without proffering a deterministic judgement. You can only do this by understanding the nature and limitations of your assessment and the processes at play when making a professional judgement.

(Kindly provided by Anne Ritchie, Dept of Social Work, University of the West of Scotland)

---

Ritchie reminds us that we are required to make professional judgements that are often necessarily limited, but that we guard against this by being aware and critically reflective about our judgements and our decisions. Ritchie suggests the following as a helpful approach to such critical reflection on risk:

1  Be aware of how you are assessing risk and the common errors influencing your judgement about risk. What biases and subjective values may be influencing you?
2  Know what your social work agency expects of your risk assessment and risk management. What is your role and responsibility?

3   Know your feelings, especially about cases and situations that are challenging and emotive, for example child neglect and abuse. What fears and emotions are you experiencing?
4   Consider the organizational and structural influences that might be impacting upon identified risk, for example, the resource constraints you are operating under and how they may impact on interventions.
5   Assess the needs, strengths and benefits of risk taking and weigh them against risk and the potential for harm and loss. Balance is important.
6   Consider all the possible interventions that may mitigate the risks presented by your risk assessment. Which interventions are the most likely to achieve the desired outcomes?
7   Ensure that you balance risk management and the personal autonomy of service users. You must always be able to justify any constraints and limits placed upon an individual and these must be proportionate to the risk and at the least intrusive level to achieve safety.
8   You must always demonstrate consideration of human rights when considering risk-management plans that may limit autonomy or the choice of the user.
   (Adapted from coursework material, Anne Ritchie, Department of Social Work, University of West of Scotland; reproduced with permission)

Intuitive reasoning and heuristics do have their place in practice. There are times when a view of risk must be formulated quickly, or where the benefit of exhaustive inquiries does not outweigh the cost (Klein 1999). In addition, in a climate of limited resources, not all cases can have equal 'thinking time' and heuristics will play an important role in moving assessment towards an intervention. The important thing to recognize is that risk assessments based largely on intuitive reasoning should be considered as *hypotheses*, in effect potentially sound but untested. It is therefore important to cultivate practice techniques to robustly test them, and to recognize where risk assessments may be partial or distorted.

---

**Activity 3.5   Testing Inductive Hypotheses on Risk**

Have you ever made a decision about risk in a hurry and then regretted it, either in your personal life or your professional work? Think about that decision now.

- Were you overly influenced by emotion and how you felt?
- Did you rely on and give too much weight to the wrong factors?
- Were you ill informed, and tempted to make the decision without knowing the full facts?

Decisions we regret are often ones we have made in haste, based on emotion and feelings, using partial or wrong information, and overlooking key information that might have helped us. So, let us consider how to improve this in future. The next time you have to reach a speedy conclusion about risk in order to develop a critical attitude, review the conclusion and the process you used to arrive at it using the following principles.

- Don't overemphasize the 'vivid, concrete, emotive, first impressions, or the most recent'.
- Don't overlook the 'dull, abstract, statistical and old'.
- Know your weaknesses and review honestly your emotional investment in the case.
- Constructively check and test your views, be evidential and seek information you do not have.
- Change your mind if required.
- Consider alternatives.
- Use line management supervision to have your assessment reviewed and tested.

(Plous 1993; Munro 1999; Slovic 2000; Kemshall et al. 2011)

As Paul and Elder put it: 'Critical thinking is . . . self-directed, self-disciplined, self-monitored, and self-corrective thinking' (2006: 4). In considering mistakes in social work, Munro concluded that:

Making mistakes can be a sign of good practice insofar as a recognition of one's fallibility is part of a general approach involving a willingness to be self-critical and to change one's mind. All social workers make many misjudgements because of the complexity of the work but skilled social workers recognize their fallibility and are open to rethinking their assessments and decisions . . . Taking a more critical attitude to one's work is not simple. It takes time, intelligence and effort. Realising your first judgements are wrong can be an unpleasant experience and social workers need to be supported and encouraged in subjecting their work to more rigorous scrutiny. Changing your mind when you receive new information or when a supervisor suggests a new way of interpreting the evidence is not a sign of weakness but of a rational, intelligent approach. (Munro 1996: 806–7)

Adopting such a self-critical, intelligent approach is the key to safe practice on risk.

## Understanding the Emotions, Values, Attitudes and Biases that Affect Decision Making in Negative Ways

The role of emotion on risk decisions has concerned psychologists, risk researchers and policy makers for some time (see Pidgeon, Kasperson and Slovic 2003 for one of the first reviews), and the impact on professionals working in the world of risk has a substantial history of investigation (Adams 1995; Carson 1996; Kemshall 1998b; Titterton 2005; Carson and Bain 2008). The studies of emotion and risk perception by Slovic are amongst the most significant (e.g. 1987, 2000). In brief, Slovic asked lay people to rank various risks ranging from nuclear accidents to disease. He found that lay people's ranking was at odds with those of experts, and that lay people ranked risks higher than the objective statistical probability of them happening. A case in point was nuclear power, with experts ranking this risk as twentieth on a list of thirty risks, based on both the number of likely fatalities and the statistical probability of the risk occurring. Lay people ranked it number one, even when the list of risks was expanded to 90. Lay people were not using the expert equation of 'risk equals probability times consequence, i.e. body count' to determine risk ranking (Gardner 2008: 76). Slovic established that other factors came into play in ranking risks, and in both public perceptions and responses to risk. These were dread (fearfulness); catastrophic consequences; involuntary risks with low personal control; likely to impact on vulnerable people (i.e. children); low trust in the experts managing the risk; and minimal benefits for the risks incurred (Slovic 1986, 1987, 2000; Lichtenstein and Slovic 2006). Slovic and his colleagues combined these into an overarching concept – the 'dread factor' – and noted the emotional response to risk this was likely to provoke (see also Pidgeon, Kasperson and Slovic 2003).

'Dread risks' also feature in social work, with child sexual offending and paedophiles being an easily recognizable example (Kitzinger 2004; Kemshall and Wood 2007, 2008). The consequences of 'dread risks' are numerous and varied. As in Slovic's research, assessors tend to inflate risk, with too much weight placed on fears of impact, with too little emphasis on probabilistic calculations of likelihood. This can lead to over-intrusion, exacerbated by defensive, back-covering practice (Baker and Wilkinson 2011). A key example is the rise in the numbers of children taken into care post the Baby Peter case and the Laming Report (2009).

### Understanding the impact of negative emotions

Conversely, 'dread risks' can lead to risk avoidance where practitioners may be challenged by risk and feel too anxious to deal with it (Slovic 2000). The result is under-intrusion and risk-management failures, literally a 'non-seeing' of risk. Risk work is therefore intrinsically emotional; feelings of fear, anxiety, stress, incompetence and paralysis are often insidious and overwhelming. In such situations, the natural tendency of practitioners is to withdraw, literally defend themselves from scrutiny. However, the impact of such negative emotions can only be managed by honesty, openness and the use of line managers to discuss how such emotions can be handled and how risk assessment can be freed from them. Consider the following reflective exercise:

---

**Activity 3.6   Reflective Exercise: Negative Emotions and Risk Assessment**

This exercise can be done using a current or recent case from your caseload, a case from a student placement, or a case study provided to students by your social work course tutor.

Consider a recent or current case where you have been affected by negative emotions.

1   List the negative emotions and what you think has led to them.
2   Be honest and list how they have impacted upon your behaviour in the case; and how they may have affected:
    a.   Your assessment of risk.
    b.   Your risk-management plans and subsequent actions in the case.
3   What help could you seek to manage these negative emotions more effectively?

---

### Understanding the impact of values and risk

Risks have to be weighed, both in terms of the likelihood of them happening, and in terms of their impact and the likely outcome of running any risk. However, as Carson and Bain put it:

Once the potential outcomes, beneficial as well as harmful, are identified, it is necessary to assign them values. It cannot simply be concluded
that a risk is worth taking just because there are more potential benefits
than there are potential harms. Nor the converse: failing to take a risk
cannot be justified just because we can think of more possible outcomes than benefits. One outcome may be so potentially harmful that
20 or more potential benefits may come nowhere close to justifying it
although . . . this can also be concluded after taking likelihood into
account. But how are we to value outcomes; where are we to find
authority for our assessments; how are we to express them? (Carson
and Bain 2008: 129)

Values are nonetheless framed and contextualized, for example by
legal requirements that govern what practitioners can and should do.
For example, child protection or mental health law in effect present
'legal values' that inform the value choices of practitioners (Carson
and Bain 2008: 131). In other arenas such as health care, competent
and adult patients can exercise choice over the risks they are prepared
to take (e.g. to have an operation or not). The value framing of desirable risks and outcomes is also rooted in professional codes of conduct
and ethical guidance. For example, in health care practitioners may
be required to concentrate on 'doing no harm' and avoiding over-
intrusion in those cases where patients are unlikely to benefit. This
does not necessarily mean that there will always be agreement
amongst health-care professionals, but it does offer a value frame and
key parameters within which individual cases can be reviewed and
debated with colleagues. As Carson and Bain put it: 'If you can demonstrate that you made a "rational" decision . . . then you should be
safe. Being able to demonstrate that you thought about, considered
and debated how to value outcomes, how you consulted colleagues,
will be seen as more "rational" than failing to do so' (2008: 136).

For example, in considering whether an older person can continue
to live independently or requires residential care, the worker has to
balance:

- autonomy versus safety of self and others;
- self-determination versus risk management;
- quality of life versus risk reduction.

Titterton reminds us that there is no such thing as a 'risk-free option'
(2005: 50). 'Welfare dilemmas' always involve difficult choices
between 'possible benefits and possible harms' and all risk decisions
involve making a choice. The key is how this decision is made, in

essence, how the balance between risk and safety is made, and the balance between risk and need is achieved. Titterton argues that it is important to be *explicit* about these balances, and to explore the choices for the client and the choices for the worker.

The following exercise encourages you to both reflect on a recent decision and to consider how you could be more explicit about how you balance risk decisions.

---

**Activity 3.7   Reflective Exercise: Balancing Risk Decisions**

Consider a recent risk decision you have made.

1   How did you value the potential outcomes of the risk?
2   How did values influence how you weighed up the decision choices open to you?
3   Which of these values were personal?
4   Which of these values would a body of responsible professional peers recognize as reasonable and applicable?
5   What consultation with colleagues or managers did you undertake or should have undertaken?

---

This exercise enables us to recognize the strong role that values can play in our decision making, sometimes without our full awareness. The outcomes we value and desire will influence the range of choices we see, and which we are likely to opt for. It is also important to recognize that some of these values will be intensely personal and may be at odds with others. For example, other workers or service users may not necessarily share these values and may come to different decisions about the same situation. This is why attempts are made to standardize values in professional codes of practice and to validate only the use of those values that a 'responsible body of peers' would recognize as reasonable and applicable to the case. Consultation is therefore critical to test this value base, especially where decisions are challenging.

These values and tensions should be clearly stated and explored, and the 'dangers' and 'advantages' to all those concerned should be expressly considered against the range of choices and interventions available (see Titterton 2005: 57). In essence, the pros and cons of differing options are weighed and risk choices are made transparent. Titterton sums this up in terms of good practice:

- clear recognition of a welfare dilemma;
- careful evaluation of arguments for and against risk taking;
- honest assessment of potential problems;
- close working with other agencies;
- engagement with clients;
- follow-up of client outcomes – how the person is coping after the risk;
- capacity for reflection. (Titterton 2005: 61–2)

Now consider how you would deal with similar dilemmas.

---

**Activity 3.8   Dealing with Risk Dilemmas**

This exercise can be done using a current or recent case from your caseload, a case from a student placement, or a case study provided to students by your social work course tutor.

Take a recent case that has presented you with a dilemma. Consider how well your practice meets the good practice criteria outlined above.

- Write down the welfare dilemma.
- List the arguments for and against risk taking.
- What are the potential problems presented by the courses of action you propose to take?
- How closely did you work with other agencies?
- How did you engage with the client and how did you explore the risk dilemma with them?
- What follow-up have you done, and with what result?
- What have you learnt from this case?

---

You may have found that the exercise makes explicit the nature of the dilemma and that rehearsing the pros and cons of risk taking is helpful in weighing up options and desirable outcomes. You may also have found that every option has costs/harms as well as benefits, and that these have to be considered and 'weighed in the balance' as you decide what to do. Considering costs and benefits also forces the social worker to consider costs, harms and benefits to whom, to prevent what risk, with what desirable outcome. As Titterton says, this requires a careful evaluation of arguments for and against risk taking. Engagement with clients is essential in order to carry out such an evaluation: do they see the dilemma as you do? What solutions are they expecting or find desirable, and why? You may wish to complete this section by considering areas where your practice does not yet match up to the good practice points outlined by Titterton, and you could identify at least one step you could take to improve your practice.

### Understanding the impact of bias and risk

We have already seen how the 'certainty/first impression bias' and the precautionary principle can affect our judgement. Decisions on risk are also prone to bias, rooted as they are in subjective inter-pretations of risk information and miscalculations of both likelihood and impact. The psychological literature on bias in risk assessment is well established (Slovic 2000), and only the main points will be covered here. Regrettably, decision errors can be commonplace, and practitioners need to know what they are and how they occur so that they can combat them (Greene and Ellis 2007; Heilbrun and Erickson 2007; Carson and Bain 2008). The key decision faults are:

- A risk decision is based on available information and further information is not actively sought. Assessment is partial and may be skewed. This is often called the availability bias.
- A causal relationship is imputed where none may actually exist. For example, there is an assumption that the use of alcohol causes violence in all cases. The association between factors, behaviours and actual risks is often not clearly explored or proven. Our thinking patterns and the associations that we make can literally lead us to see 'causes' of risk that do not really exist.
- The likelihood of a risk is estimated against an erroneous start-ing point, for example, one based on the practitioner's experi-ence of similar cases. However, such cases may be rare within the population as a whole, although more common on the practitioner's caseload. This can bias the assessment of likeli-hood because the practitioner weighs the risk against their personal starting point and not against the base rate in the population as a whole.
- Hindsight bias and the operation of the precautionary princi-ple. Practitioners and managers can overreact to risk-management failures and apply the luxury of hindsight to failures when judging decisions. This can result in a precaution-ary response to cases and clients of a similar type.

- Practitioners can over-rely on their personal and professional experience. This can lead practitioners to see similarity in cases that do not actually exist, and to weigh new situations within the parameters and value frames of previous cases rather than assessing situations and clients 'as new'. This is called the representative bias.
- Practitioners select and use the information which confirms and reinforces the decision and course of action that they have already chosen. This is the confirmation bias.
- Unrealistic optimism. Practitioners see case improvement, change and progress, although the weight of evidence for this may actually be small. Practitioners work hard to achieve change, and consequently invest small changes with a greater significance than they actually deserve. This can result in risk minimization.
- Overemphasizing benefits when presenting risk information to others. For example, parole boards may weigh the benefit of release under parole supervision as a key benefit over continued custody, and weigh this higher than the likelihood of reoffending on release, based upon current reconviction rates for that type of crime and offender. (Tversky and Kahneman 1974; Kahneman, Slovic and Tversky 1990; Strachan and Tallant 1997; Slovic 2000; Tavris and Aaronson 2007; Carson and Bain 2008; Hollows 2008; Kemshall 2008b)

Practitioners cannot be completely free from bias. All assessors bring with them their beliefs, their emotional responses and their ways of thinking about the world and these individual differences will interact with different environmental contexts. It is critical that practitioners can reflect on their own biases and take corrective action, and that their managers can help them do so. The following exercise helps you to identify bias in your own practice.

---

### Activity 3.9   Exercise on Bias

Here are some examples of the biases mentioned above. Fill in a blank table with your own examples. You may find it useful to use this exercise in classroom settings, on student placements or to review your own practice. Managers or supervisors can use this with teams and their staff.

| Source of Bias | Example |
|---|---|
| Practitioner value base. | Believing that some clients have no right to be helped because of what they have done. Believing that all children are better off at home than in care. |
| Conscious or unconscious discrimination (whether class, gender, race, sexuality, beliefs about the proper demeanour of the interviewee and so on). | Believing that black people are naturally more likely to be aggressive. Believing that single mothers are 'poor mothers'. |
| Use of invalid models: for example, an understanding of behaviour drawn from the media rather than from properly researched evidence. | Believing that the majority of sex offenders target children who are strangers to them. Believing that victims of domestic violence never leave. |
| The beliefs of the assessor in his/her (in)ability to work effectively with a particular client or client group. | Thinking that you do not have the skills to work with clients who are racist, so leaving that work undone. Doubting your ability to challenge violent behaviour successfully so these behaviours aren't targeted for change. Doubting that you can change established patterns of inappropriate parenting behaviour – behaviours go unchallenged. |
| Unreal optimism: wanting to believe you are being effective and that an individual is making progress. | A client has attended a group regularly and cooperated fully, e.g. a parenting group, alcohol group, etc. You do not want to hear information that suggests they have continued their problematic behaviour outside the group. |
| Unreal pessimism: refusing to see signs of progress. | A client makes real changes and progress, but because this client and others have relapsed so often in the past, you doubt the genuineness of this change. |

| Source of Bias | Example |
| --- | --- |
| You overestimate your abilities and likely impact on the behaviour and choices of the client. | You uncritically expect that clients will do as instructed or asked. You expect your advice to be taken without fully considering the motivation, reluctance or expectations of the client. The client then 'fails' to comply and you are angry and disappointed. You waste resources setting up referrals and access to services that the client does not use. This presents you and your agency in a poor light with these services. At worst, you fail to see that the client is making little progress and that risk is increasing. |
| Being afraid of an individual client. | A client is threatening and intimidating. You are fearful and uncomfortable. You keep visits to a minimum, you do not ask investigative or challenging questions and you do not challenge inappropriate comments or behaviours. |
| Representative: assuming knowledge of one client of a particular group means you know about all clients in that group. | You work with a sex offender who repeatedly lies and lets you down. You assume that all sex offenders will be the same. You have experience of a mentally ill client becoming violent. You assume that all mentally ill persons are prone to violence. |
| Confirmation: only paying attention to information that supports the judgement you have already reached. | You decide that a woman victim of domestic abuse is over-emotional and prone to exaggerating. When information reaches you that she is being abused again, you minimize its significance. |
| Availability: over-reliance on information easily obtained. | You don't seek information from others but rely instead on old reports and your own interview. |

(Adapted from Wilkinson 2011)

Managers and supervisors can also use this exercise with their staff to identify the most common biases and to help staff develop self-reflection on their decision making.

## Alternative Frameworks for Decision Making:
## Rehearsing Risk Scenarios

As Webb has eloquently stated: 'Social work is dogged by risk and the unexpected' (2002: 48). Practitioners are required to make decisions under conditions of uncertainty, with little time and often in less than optimal circumstances. In addition, 'decisions in social work are always contaminated by complexities which are influenced by organizational, political and economic interests' (Webb 2002: 49). Social work decisions often involve the unpredictable, unexpected and the complex. As Webb suggests, the main problems associated with making effective decisions in social work include:

- risk and uncertainty;
- intangibles (often in social work risk assessments we are grappling with issues and problems that have not fully developed or formed; they are literally 'difficult to grasp');
- multiple criteria (for example, some assessments require us to balance criteria for personal autonomy against criteria for personal safety);
- long-term implications;
- interdisciplinary input and the politics of vested interest;
- pooled decision making;
- value judgements. (Webb 2002: 52)

These are particularly acute in risk decisions.

In other professions, decision analysis and the use of risk scenarios have gained some ground in dealing with these difficulties (for example, the nuclear industry, engineering, environmental risk management and health care). In brief, decision analysis attempts to make the risks and the probabilities of outcomes associated with any decision explicit. The practitioner explicitly considers the differing risk scenarios, the likelihood of them occurring, the possible outcomes and harms, and the possible responses, and the impact of possible responses not only on the risk but on the service user, and on significant others. In other words, the risk assessor considers a number of risk scenarios along the lines of: 'if X happens, then Y will result, but if A happens, then B might result.' These differing risk scenarios can also be weighted in terms of the probability of them actually occurring (or being chosen), and in terms of the desirability of any likely outcome. For example, such a technique could be applied when considering residential care for an older person in a situation where issues of self-harm and potential harm to others is likely but where the older person values their independence and quality of life. Differing options can be rehearsed with likely outcomes considered and reviewed, for example, the consequences for service users of moving into residential care and the likely impact on their quality of life, well-being and longevity. Risk scenario planning is discussed in more detail in chapter 4.

This technique gives the practitioner some space to rehearse likely outcomes from decisions, and compare and contrast which are the most desirable, to whom, and why. It can also enable practitioners to weigh the actual probability that an outcome will arise, and the weight of evidence for that, for example the relative probabilities of harm arising from leaving an abused child at home as against residential care, fostering or adoption. Munro has shown how evidence-based probabilities of harm can be calculated for each of these options based on child protection research (2008a: 147–52). Such decisions can be life-changing and life-protecting, and as such are far from simple:

> In child welfare, we rarely face a simple choice between a good and bad consequence. All carry a mixture of pros and cons. Leaving children with their birth parents has many benefits as well as some risk of abuse; moving them to a new home carries greater safety but also many risks of broken attachments. Money also plays a part in weighting the utility value since it is a finite resource. A program of support may increase the probability of safe care for one child but make such resource demands that it limits help for other families. (Munro 2008a: 197)

In this way, evidence for options can be used to inform risk decisions where complex values and competing perspectives of different agencies (and clients) may alter decision making inappropriately. This can assist practitioners to avoid 'tunnel vision' and seeing decision choices in terms of a simple binary 'either/or' (Munro 2008a: 197). The method promotes analytic reasoning and enables practitioners to make their intuitive judgements explicit. The method is also important for enabling practitioners to formally consider contingencies, and encouraging a structured focus on the 'what ifs' of the case. Munro acknowledges that applying decision analysis requires time and effort and is therefore best suited to major decisions and those that have long-term significance. Such decisions must also pass the test of hindsight scrutiny and defensibility and Munro suggests that decision analysis is likely to result in more defensible decisions (2008a).

While this approach has become increasingly common in health care (Elwyn, Edwards, Eccles and Rovner 2001), it has yet to make a significant impact on social work. This is due in part to difficulties perceived in the translation from the health arena to the social work one (Webb 2002), and formal probability thinking is still largely eschewed in social work. Despite this, risk scenarios can be useful for prompting practitioners to consider alternative options, comparing the range of likely and desirable outcomes arising from different courses of action, and to be explicit about the values assigned to particular risk outcomes.

## Conclusion

This chapter has focused on the 'art of decision making', looking at how 'good judgement' can be hampered and how to develop better practice when making risk decisions. Decisions are only as good as the practitioners making them, and this chapter has outlined the key pitfalls for practitioners. Knowing pitfalls doesn't always mean you can avoid them, but it is an important first step. Adopting and using the techniques presented here can help to reduce the likelihood and impact of decision errors. Alternative ways of making decisions, such as rehearsing risk scenarios, can also assist practitioners to weigh up options more explicitly, to rehearse possible consequences of their decisions and to consider contingency plans. Finally, overall risk systems are only as good as the quality assurance systems that maintain and improve them. Failure to quality assure will, at some time, result in failure – this issue will be further discussed in chapter 6.

### FURTHER READING

Hollows, A. (2008) 'Professional judgement and the risk assessment process,' in M. Calder (ed.), *Contemporary Risk Assessment in Safeguarding Children*. Lyme Regis: Russell House Publishing, pp. 52–60. Largely written from a child protection perspective, this has a wider applicability to practice with a range of service users. The importance of professional judgement is emphasized within the context of good practice.

Lehrer, J. (2009) *The Decision Moment: How the Brain Makes up its Mind*. New York: Canongate. This is an entertaining book, focusing on how and why we make decision errors about risk. By using a range of examples, the book illustrates the many decision traps that risk assessors are likely to fall into. An informative and enjoyable read.

Titterton, M. (2005) *Risk and Risk Taking in Health and Social Welfare.* London: Jessica Kingsley Publishers. This is an excellent introduction to decision making about risk in the caring professions. The style is accessible, with helpful practical examples.

# 4

# *Risk Planning and Management*

Risk assessment and management are interlinked activities and planning for risk requires practitioners to make explicit links between the two processes. In order to reduce risk, the plans that are made and acted upon must flow from a balanced, evidence-based risk assessment. As chapter 2 spelt out, the purpose of risk assessment includes being very clear about the risks that the assessor is concerned with and the circumstances and conditions that may increase or decrease risk. In order to be clear, the assessment should specify:

- the risk factors that are present and their potential links with harmful outcomes;
- positive factors and their potential for reducing harm.

Risk assessments should be specific to the individuals concerned, their diversity and circumstances and the social work context within which the assessment is taking place; so too should risk-management planning. When reading someone else's risk-assessment and management plan, the reader should be able to clearly understand:

- the strategies that have been selected;
- how they have emerged from the risk assessment;
- how they link to desired outcomes.

Risk-management planning should be focused and structured, producing plans that balance a clear sense of direction with the ability to be flexible. Plans should clearly outline roles and responsibilities which should be communicated to the individuals concerned. Trotter (2002) calls this process role clarification, an essential skill. In a study of the reunification of looked-after children with their families, Farmer, Sturgess and O'Neill (2008) found more stable returns where there was preparation as part of a planned return and the support given was purposeful and proactive. This planned approach reduced the risk that children would suffer abuse on return to the family, or be damaged by unnecessary movements between home and care.

Figure 1.1 in chapter 1 summarized the stages of the assessment process. The current chapter works through a structured approach to risk management looking in more detail at the planning, delivery and review stages already identified. Before embarking on these stages, a risk assessment should indicate if risk-management planning is appropriate and at what level and we begin with a consideration of how that decision is made. The chapter will conclude with a consideration of working with others in the context of risk management.

## Thresholds and Categorization

Thresholds were briefly considered in chapter 2. A key first decision resulting from a risk assessment is whether or not a particular individual or individuals, in a specific set of circumstances, gives rise to sufficient concern to reach the threshold for a designated level of intervention. Estimations of likelihood and imminence and the possible extent and nature of harm will inform decisions about thresholds. When services can and should be delivered will be enshrined in policy, but are also a matter of judgement about individuals and circumstances. Chapter 2 introduced the implications of false positives and false negatives in risk assessment, and their significance for risk management is also clear.

- If thresholds are set too high, they will increase the numbers of those categorized as not eligible to receive a needed service and, for some, the likelihood and extent of harm may be increased as a result. Analyses of child deaths and serious injury have found that the children concerned were often not subject to formal safeguarding procedures (Brandon et al. 2008a). Widespread concerns have been documented about the high proportion of 'at risk' cases not 'deemed to be of sufficiently high priority to be allocated resources' (Driscoll 2009: 336). It is 'important that services are available to support the needs of vulnerable children and young people who are not in need of protection but who clearly need help' (Munro 2011: 81).

- If thresholds are too low, then more individuals and families will be subject to interventions that may restrict their liberty and cause significant distress. Unnecessary and disproportionate interventions are more likely when there is an overemphasis on low-probability, high-cost events (e.g. child deaths). Large numbers of unnecessary referrals skew the allocation of resources and attention, so that again preventative work may be under-resourced and the capacity to provide services to those most likely to suffer serious harm may be diminished (Munro 2008b; Macdonald and Macdonald 2010; Munro 2011).

Thresholds, at whatever level, can have a significant impact on the experiences of individuals and families and also on relationships and decision making between agencies. Commentators have suggested that, in the context of child protection, there has been too mechanistic an approach and an overemphasis on whether the criteria for a particular threshold have been reached (Brandon et al. 2008b; Devaney 2008). High thresholds of eligibility for children's services can make other professionals feel powerless to intervene (Brandon, Dodsworth and Rumball 2005).

Categorization, i.e. assigning individuals or families to particular groups, is often the formal (and informal) result of an assessment and will inform decision making about thresholds. For example, an individual is assigned to a particular risk category; this then crosses the threshold for intervention. Less formal categorizations of individuals and families also make a difference to the nature of the service provided. A report on serious case reviews points out that, for young people over the age of 14, agencies were seeing them as hard to reach or rebellious, which meant that workers did not seek to understand the causes of their behaviour and need for support (Ofsted 2011). Young people were put into a category that could fundamentally affect the service received without those who were engaged in that categorization necessarily making an explicit decision. Rochdale Borough Safeguarding Children's Board (2012: 11) found that 'behaviours indicative of sexual exploitation were seen rather as problematic, and essentially wilful, behaviours on the part of the child; . . .

Older children were considered to have capacity to make their own decisions and were not perceived to be as "at risk" of harm as younger children.' Hall and Slembrouck (2009) suggest that processes like case conferences are driven by categorization (sometimes implicit) and their associated justifications. This brings with it a set of role expectations for all involved and implications for how effectively agencies can work together.

Categorization that is rooted in avoiding and reducing risk may also result in failure to pay the right balance of attention to the benefits of taking risks. Bornat and Bytheway (2010) suggest that risk-averse practice can promote and reinforce images of older people as passive and dependent. They point out that risk should be a negotiation, entailing compromise, where the freedom of older people to take risks should be considered as an important part of the balance. The minimization of risk needs to be balanced against the preferences of the older person for independence and the wishes and needs of family members and concerned others. Manthorpe and Moriarty (2010), discussing risk enablement, support the importance of negotiation with individuals with dementia so that a shared understanding of risk can be arrived at.

---

### Activity 4.1   Thresholds and Categorization

Consider the following example which could also be discussed, in a group, as part of teaching or training.

A case conference is deciding what action needs to be taken to safeguard a 15-year-old girl who is working as a street prostitute. The professional participants in the discussion see the child in the way that young people were viewed in Bradford (see p. 73). How might that perception make a difference to the services delivered for that young person?

If you have current or recent experience in a practice setting, you could also think about the ways in which service users are categorized in that setting. How do those judgements affect:

* how the case is seen by practitioners?
* how agencies communicate and work with each other and with service users?
* the service delivered?

Note specific implications for practice that you have been able to identify.

---

## Key Stages in Planning and Delivering Risk Management

This chapter will take you through the elements of planned and proactive risk management, breaking down the stages of planning delivery and review, in cases where the risk of harm is significant. Key components of a planned approach are summarized in the table below.

| A planned approach to risk management | |
|---|---|
| Goal | Reducing likelihood of specific harms, risk reduction |
| | Positive outcomes |
| What needs to change | Risk factors to be removed, or reduced<br>Positive risks to be taken<br>Strengths to be developed |
| How change will be brought about | Restrictive measures<br>Constructive measures<br>Service-user participation |
| Timescales and sequencing | Imminence<br>Steps to change |
| Contingency planning | Planning for escalation or deterioration<br>Making the most of positive opportunities |
| Recording, monitoring and review | Process |
| | Outcomes |

As you look at the table above, think about what your immediate response is. Does it seem overwhelming, given the number of tasks that are included? Do you wonder how all those different components can be brought together in a coherent plan? One thing that will help in bringing apparently disparate elements together is that, of course, these components interact with and influence each other, rather than standing alone. This adds to the complexity of planning but, if done well, it also helps the process become more practical and focused. Each of these components is now considered in more detail.

## The Goal of Risk Management

Fundamentally, risk management should seek to reduce the likelihood of harmful outcomes occurring, or, if they do still occur, reducing the degree of harm likely to be caused. The outcomes of concern will of course be influenced by the practice context, so different considerations will apply in working with older people, people with learning difficulties or with children, for example. In relation to mental health and risk, Maden is unequivocal about interventions reducing risk, arguing 'that is why risk management matters: treatment can make a difference' (2011: 104). In whatever context, the goals of risk management should not be poorly defined but should be specific, relevant and realistic. Risk-management goals should specify both the risks that are being addressed and the positive outcomes that are being sought.

Sometimes the outcomes being sought conflict with each other. The reduction of a set of risks may result in the restriction of the rights, liberty and activities of individuals (Kemshall 2008b). Reducing the risk of harm to a child, for example, may entail restrictions on the rights of that child's parents, the child themselves and other family members. Reducing the risk of harm to an older person may restrict that person's freedom of choice; on the other hand, allowing them more opportunity to take the risks they choose may impact on the freedom of others who are responsible for caring for them (Bornat and Bytheway 2010).

In a discussion of care planning and review for looked-after children, Thomas (2011) highlights that the primary aim of the planning and review system should be to safeguard and promote children's welfare. He also notes that secondary aims of stability – reducing impermanence, allowing appropriate family contact, making transparent decisions and including children – should support and overlap with the primary aim but that sometimes in practice it can be hard to bring those aims together coherently.

---

**Activity 4.2  Balancing Risk Reduction against Potential Negative Outcomes**

A father is found to be downloading child pornography, but at this stage there is no evidence of abusive behaviour to his own children. Consider how you might seek to answer some of the questions below in order to balance risk reduction against the negative impact of any action taken.

- Should the father be removed from the home while an assessment is made when there is no direct victim?

- What is the likelihood of harm to the children of the family if he remains?
- What is the impact on family life of the father's removal? Is it proportionate?
- If removal of the father from the home does take place, should all contact with the children be suspended, given the subtlety of grooming which could be taking place even during supervised access?
- Whatever decisions are made, how can they be explained to non-abused children?

As the activity illustrates, balancing needs, rights and responsibilities can be difficult. To begin to answer some of the questions posed in the activity, you would need to engage with all the family members, finding out about family relationships and how everyone involved understands their situation. You would also need far more information about the father's activities and about any other agency involvement with that family. There is a fundamental responsibility to reduce harm to the individuals subject to a plan and to others. However, risk will always involve a degree of uncertainty. It is not possible to remove all risk and so the focus should be on reducing the likelihood and impact of harm in a proportionate way. Intervention should take place only at a level that is justified by the degree of risk (Kemshall 2010b).

Reducing harm is not a sufficient goal for social work involvement with families and individuals. The individuals with whom social workers engage have a right to a positive quality of life, not just a life where risks are under control. Also, risk management both for adults and children should not, if at all possible, be experienced as a negative process. Instead, it should be delivered in a way that promotes the active involvement of service users and has specific positive outcomes (Barnett and Mann 2011). This active involvement is important because it makes a difference to how the person who is subject to risk management views the experience, helping that individual to feel more able to influence decision making and also potentially making them more likely to share relevant information with the risk manager. In turn, this can help to improve risk management and ensure that interventions are more relevant to individual lives and circumstances. It may also make a difference to the extent to which subjects can be helped to take more responsibility for their own lives.

Incorporating risk taking in plans can support the development of capacity – skills and social capital – amongst service users. There can be a 'tendency to overlook the importance of competence, coping, capacity and capital' (Titterton 2011: 32). He suggests that improvements in individual and social capital may be very significant for long-term risk reduction and may increase motivation to engage. Motivated individuals are more likely to comply with attempts to change risky behaviours and situations and to play an active part in living with and managing their own risks. Goals that develop strengths and that may entail positive risk taking also need to be part of planning and to be as purposeful as the goals addressing risk factors. All the goals in a plan should be clearly linked to the overall purpose and relevant to the particular needs and circumstances of the individual, or individuals, concerned.

---

**Activity 4.3     Balances in Risk-Management Plans**

The following questions can be asked about a plan in a work setting or placement. They could be used in supervision or in team development to review planning practice. The questions are to be asked of a plan which sets out what should be achieved by specific interventions:

- To what extent is the plan explicit about both risk reduction and positive outcomes for service users?
- Is there evidence that service users were actively involved in putting together the plan?
- How appropriately does the plan balance any restrictions aimed at risk reduction with the rights of those concerned?
- Having considered the answers to the above questions, how might the plan be improved?

---

## What Needs to Change?

The detailed contents of a plan should then reflect the changes that need to be made to achieve harm reduction and positive outcomes. The plan should seek to change significant risk factors that have been identified in the assessment, as well as to support and develop existing strengths. Risk factors and strengths may reside in the individual who is the focus of risk management, and/or within the family or wider context, so both individual and contextual interventions will need to be considered. This may be challenging because social work tasks have become more fragmented, making it more difficult for practitioners to build expertise in using contextual information (Burton and Van den Broeck 2009). If, for example, different members of staff are taking referral information from those who complete the subsequent in-depth assessment, vital contextual clues at the initial point of crisis might be missed.

Taking into account differences in context is particularly important to enable appropriate responses to diverse individuals and communities. Studies around the abuse of older people have not identified systemic culturally based differences in black and minority ethnic (BME) communities. BME communities are influenced by generational and gender differences as are others and groups and individuals within each community will also have their own experiences and views. Studies indicate some differences in BME communities' views about the care of older people and the nature and causes of abuse and these views should be taken into account in risk planning. For example, the influence of culture and the experience of racism may both be relevant and may interact. 'With few exceptions we found that services for BME older people had limited knowledge of adult protection issues, and adult protection services, with limited exceptions, had paid scant attention to issues for BME communities' (Bowes, Avan and Mackintosh 2008: 93). Hollomotz (2009) supports the importance of context, suggesting that an ecological model for understanding risk is important. For example, people with learning difficulties are more likely to be subject to sexual violence. In order to intervene to reduce the likelihood of abuse, it is important to think about all of the causes of that violence, both individual and contextual. For this group, an over-individualized focus on risk may prevent positive risk taking, for example allowing them the chance to practise their own independent decision making. Without this, they may remain more at risk from the behaviour of others because they haven't had the chance to develop skills in keeping themselves safe. A proper understanding of context, in this case, means that positive risk taking may be an important strategy for risk reduction.

Addressing risk factors while also supporting strengths is not the only complexity in deciding where to focus change efforts. Many risk factors for harmful behaviour are long-standing; they may have originated much earlier in life, and they may be difficulties that the person has been struggling with over a long period of time. These predisposing risk factors mean that some individuals and situations bring with them a higher likelihood of harmful outcomes. Long-standing isolation in older people, for example, may make a harmful outcome more likely. For this outcome to occur, however, there are likely to be other more immediate risk factors of great significance. These more immediate triggers to particular kinds of behaviours or incidents interact with predisposing issues so that harmful events are more likely to take place. An older person may cope, over time, in a situation of isolation and be able to survive independently, but a health crisis, or urgent practical difficulties, could result in a much increased likelihood of a seriously harmful outcome. On the other hand, someone may have predisposing risk factors from experiences in early childhood but have current strengths that make a harmful outcome less likely, for example, a successful foster placement.

---

**Activity 4.4   Different Kinds of Risk Factors**

Think about a case with which you are familiar or use the case study in Activity 3.3. For your own case or for the study, list both individual and contextual:

- predisposing risk factors;
- more immediate triggers;
- strengths.

How do they interact with and influence each other? How might a plan address each of these?

---

What is also essential in accurately choosing the right areas for intervention is to select those most likely to make a difference to outcomes. A risk plan must be rooted in an evidence-based understanding of causal patterns. These causal patterns help us understand what is leading to the potential harmful behaviour or situation. This is more than a list of risk factors because the mere existence of a risk factor does not of itself guide action (Munro 2010a). Figure 2.1 on p. 27 is a simple diagram used to think through a range of risk factors, their interactions with each other and with the harmful outcome in order to explore direct and indirect causes of harm. To decide on what changes interventions hope to achieve, it is necessary to think in more depth about how particular factors are linked directly, or

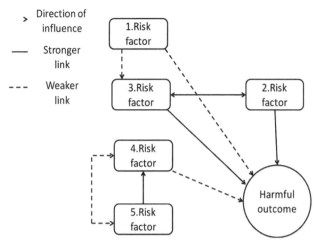

**Figure 4.1** Strength of interactions between risk factors

indirectly, to the goals of risk management. In Figure 4.1, we take the earlier approach a little further in considering not just the existence of links and interrelationships, but also the strengths of those influences.

You can see that some risk factors are mutually influential, some have strong influences, others weaker ones, on the harmful outcome; some have only indirect influence, some direct. In a particular case, risk management requires the precise nature of those causal links to be understood. For example, if substance misuse in a parent is a strong influence on risk to a child, in what way is that operating? Is it because the substance misuse directly affects their parenting ability, or is it because the substance misuse makes a difference to other behavioural choices, for example violent behaviour?

---

**Activity 4.5   Thinking about the Strengths and Directions of Influence**

The approach used in Figure 4.1 can be used to analyse any case by writing out risk factors and then drawing lines to illustrate your judgements about the strengths, nature and direction of influence. It could be used for a current case or as an activity on a case study, as part of training or teaching.

- Draw out the risk factors and strengths as illustrated in Figure 4.1 for your chosen case. It would also be very helpful to briefly note on your diagram what evidence you have for the judgements you are making about influence. Does this process make a difference to any of the judgements you have arrived at?
- In the same case, use a parallel approach but this time, instead of risk factors, identify positive factors and think about the nature and strength of their influence in protecting against harmful outcomes.

You could use this approach in an interview with a service user if it seemed appropriate. If you ask them to help you draw up the risks and/ or positives and strengths of influence, do they see them in the same terms as involved professionals?

Having identified influences, strengths and patterns of interaction, you then need to think about which of the influences are most amenable to change as this will realistically inform the contents of any plan. Not all desirable changes can be achieved; achievements may be limited by resources and by the skills, capacities and circumstances of those concerned. Sometimes changes require the active and willing involvement of other family members, for example, to enable a child at risk to remain safely at home. It is important to be realistic about the motivation of those concerned. For example, apparent or disguised cooperation from parents could delay an understanding of the severity of harm to a child (Brandon et al. 2008a). It is also important that the motivation to engage isn't seen as fixed but as potentially varying over time. Developing motivation to change can itself be an important goal of intervention (Darlington, Healy and Feeney 2010).

Changes that are sought need to be realistic and likely to make a difference to outcomes. They need to be rooted in an understanding of possible causality. They should engage the active participation of those involved and at the same time remain questioning about the substance of apparent motivation to change.

## How Will Change be Brought About?

Having identified goals and targets for change, the next stage is to make decisions about how to intervene and what strategies to use in order to bring about the changes that are most likely to reduce risk. Her Majesty's Inspectorate of Probation (HMIP) (2009) use the terms 'restrictive' and 'constructive' to broadly divide types of risk-management strategies.

- Restrictive strategies are sometimes necessary in order to exercise control over the ability of individuals to behave in certain ways or to make particular decisions. A young person on release from custody may be subject to a curfew, or to a condition that they live at a particular address. Restrictions may be very important, particularly in managing immediate risks or helping to make the situation safer, so that other strategies can be put in place. Restrictive strategies have significant limitations, however. They are often very costly and impractical to sustain in the long term and they have very significant implications for freedoms and rights. It is therefore much harder to keep an appropriate proportional balance if restrictive measures dominate.

- Constructive strategies do more than merely control. They are directed at helping to change individual characteristics and specific circumstances that make a negative event more likely. They require motivation from those who are subject to them and a degree of engagement with the process of change. If this can be achieved, more long-lasting risk reduction is likely and will be more effective in bringing about real behavioural and attitudinal change. Constructive strategies can also be directed at building and supporting strengths and positive circumstances.

When asking others to take or to avoid certain behaviours, the practitioner is exercising a degree of power. The kind of power relationship being drawn upon is linked to the balance between restrictive and constructive interventions. Repressive power aimed at producing compliance with risk-management strategies is sometimes necessary, perhaps as the first stage in change (Ericson 2007). If someone fails to keep appointments or to comply with the minimum demands of monitoring arrangements, then risk management cannot take place. On its own, however, repressive power is likely at best to achieve formal compliance, rather than substantive engagement and change (Robinson and McNeill 2008). Productive power, in contrast, involves the person who is subject to that power as a stakeholder in the process. In other words, they are convinced that changes will bring about real benefits, for example, an improved ability to care for their children. They have a more substantive motivation for keeping appointments, or complying with monitoring, and change is therefore more likely to be embedded (Ericson 2007).

A comprehensive risk-management plan will therefore appropriately combine restrictive and constructive strategies. The exact balance may depend on the likelihood, potential impact and imminence of the possible risk and on the motivation of those who are subject to the plan.

In addition, individual strategies of whatever kind cannot be considered in isolation. Instead, they must be chosen because they complement and support each other. Figure 4.2 shows layers of risk strategies and suggests that most strategies will inevitably contain gaps (Reason 2008). Other layers of strategies are needed to 'plug' the gaps and produce more comprehensive protection and likelihood of positive change.

Think about the following situation where Marcia, aged nine, is at risk because of neglect, linked to alcohol misuse by her mother, Kay. Marcia misses school, or arrives dirty and sometimes hungry. Her behaviour is deteriorating and she is becoming isolated from other children.

- The layer at the top of the diagram represents strategies that require the active engagement of Kay in managing her own drinking behaviour. These strategies include the provision of help from an alcohol agency. She is also going to receive support to help her increase the standards of child care she provides. The gaps in this top layer suggest that in this instance, while Kay has real motivation to change, the extent of the problem means that this is unlikely to be sufficiently sustained to be effective on its own.
- A second layer of strategies includes the development of Kay's personal strengths. These strategies will support her

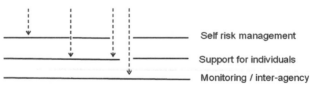

Self risk management

Support for individuals

Monitoring / inter-agency

**Figure 4.2**   Model of combined risk strategies and gaps

motivation and confidence and provide positive feedback on her developing standards of child care. There will also be behavioural work for Marcia and Kay individually, with some work together, aimed at improving Kay's exercise of appropriate engagement with Marcia and her ability to set boundaries. The work with Marcia will improve her skills with other children and her ability to respond constructively to boundary setting.

- If this is still not judged to be sufficient, another level of strategy is needed. This involves regular monitoring of both child and mother and regular communication between agencies. Practitioners will be watching out for any developing risk factors, such as heavy drinking from Kay, or a disengagement from services that may jeopardize progress or suggest that a harmful event is becoming more imminent. Regular communication will enable a prompt response.

Of course, like any diagram, this is over-simplistic. It implies that with sufficient layers, absolute control is possible and that every layer is so clearly identifiable and distinct. Reality is more complicated but it does draw attention to the fact that all the strategies are important and that they have to be considered as a whole. Of course, even if absolute control were possible, it would still be important to bear in mind proportionality. The task therefore remains to put in place proportional strategies which reduce the risk of gaps in protection to a realistic minimum. The following activity asks you to give this some more thought.

---

### Activity 4.6   Layers of Risk Strategies

Look back at the example above:

- Make a list of all of the strategies described and, as the diagram suggests, make a note of the ways in which they reduce risk and of the gaps in the protection they offer.
- Does the range of strategies help to compensate for gaps? Are there gaps unfilled?
- Note which of these strategies are predominantly restrictive and which constructive.
- Note which of the strategies support strengths.

- Are you happy with the overall balances between restrictive and constructive strategies and between addressing risks and supporting strengths?

Having done the above activity, Figure 4.2 could also be used to analyse the strategies in an active case. Looking at the detail of a risk-management plan, use the following procedure to analyse it:

- Make a list of all of the strategies.
- Take each strategy in turn and identify the gaps which might make a risky outcome still likely to occur.
- Do the strategies support strengths and address relevant risk factors?
- Does the range of strategies do a good job in compensating gaps?
- Finally, is this plan proportionate to the degree and likelihood of harm anticipated? Are any changes to the plan necessary?

So how do we know what balance of interventions to use in which situation? Where the likelihood of a significant harmful event is high, more restrictive strategies may be judged to be proportionate. They are often more central when there is a lack of motivation to engage, for example if someone's mental health deteriorates significantly and they are unable, or unwilling, to positively engage with services. As Maden (2011) points out, practitioners in the field of mental health commonly work with clients who, when well, pose a low risk of violence, but whose risk is much higher when they relapse. In some cases, mental health relapse can outweigh all other factors, at least in the short term where it may pose an imminent risk. In such cases, restrictive interventions, sometimes involving loss of liberty, may be necessary. Of course, such interventions carry with them concerns for human rights so regular reviews and adaptation to changing circumstances are also crucial.

How restrictive strategies are delivered is important. The boundaries between what is restrictive and what is constructive are not always clear-cut. Restrictive strategies can, for example, provide the breathing space needed for engagement with other constructive interventions. They are more likely to be experienced positively and complied with if delivered with care and sensitivity. There is some evidence in work with offenders who are subject to enforced interventions for substance misuse that it is not the coercion itself that is of significance but how it is perceived. This can be influenced by the skills of the workers concerned (Hough 1996). If restrictive power is clearly exercised in order to help achieve desired goals, then it is more likely to be accepted.

There is a difficult balance in child protection between supporting parents and at the same time focusing on the risks to children (Forrester et al. 2008b). In their study of interviewing skills used by social workers, Forrester et al. found a significant level of confrontational approaches in workers responding to concerns about risk. They suggest that the goal of reducing risks to children, while central, may have unhelpfully distorted the understanding of practitioners about the skills they should apply to achieve that goal. As a result, too inquisitorial a style dominated, rather than the use of 'reflecting back' skills which may be more effective. Trotter (2002) points out the importance of role clarification here. Social workers need to be clear about their overall responsibility without losing sight of the skills in communication and engagement that are likely to help achieve outcomes.

The aim of participatory practice is to achieve effective risk management ethically. Where possible, service users should be involved in selecting both the goals and the methods for achieving them, but it isn't always straightforward to involve family members in decision making (Darlington, Healy and Feeney 2010). A number of things may make a difference to how practical it can be. For example, in child protection, parental willingness to understand their children's needs is critical. Without that, there may be real conflicts between the goals of participative practice and child protection. To enable meaningful participation, practitioners need to exercise skill and take the necessary time to establish a useful relationship. In a consideration of the 2005 Mental Capacity Act, McDonald suggests that debates that have been generated are concerned with 'the extent to which older people are truly supported in making complex decisions and choices about how they live their lives. Barriers, both structural and organizational, to positive risk-taking . . . need to be considered' (2010b: 1243).

In order to actively engage service users in changing their behaviour or circumstances, it has been found helpful to maximize the use of positive goals. Approach goals rather than avoidance goals are more likely to bring about successful change (Beech and Mann 2002; Farrow, Kelly and Wilkinson 2007; Barnett and Mann 2011).

An approach goal is positive and active and involves working towards something, whereas an avoidance goal is about stopping or avoiding, which is more negative and passive in focus. For example:

- An avoidance goal is 'I am not going to eat chocolate biscuits when I get in from work.'
- An approach goal is 'I am going to eat at least two pieces of fruit when I get home before I eat anything else.'

The avoidance goal means that, even if you eat no biscuits for a week, the day that you have a single biscuit, you have failed and you haven't learned anything as a result of your efforts. The approach goal means that, even if sometimes you still have a biscuit, you are likely to eat fewer than previously and you have acquired a new and positive behaviour as a fruit eater. Far more opportunities for success are built in and you have learned something as a result of your efforts. (Baker, Kelly and Wilkinson 2011: 95)

Approach goals help service users increase their sense of efficacy, their skills and their ability to put those skills into practice to achieve desired outcomes (Bandura 1997).

---

### Activity 4.7   Writing Approach Goals

You could take a real case and write out the goals for change that were agreed with the service user. For each of these goals, answer the following:

- Was it expressed as an approach or an avoidance goal?
- If the latter, have a go at rewriting it in more positive approach-based terms. Alternatively, go back to the case that was used in Activity 4.6.
- Have a go at writing some goals for Kay and Marcia that are expressed in approach terms.

How does the use of approach goals make it more likely that service users can learn from their achievement?

---

## Timescales and Sequencing

Having decided what needs to change and how to go about seeking that change, interventions then have to be delivered in practice in a planned way, agreed as far as possible with service users.

Before looking in more detail at some of the elements of a staged approach, it is important to acknowledge that plans sometimes have to be changed. For example, there will be occasions where one pressing risk factor, or a combination of risk factors, produces a situation of imminent risk and it may be necessary to take immediate action. Such actions might include taking a child to a place of safety or moving an adult from their own home into institutional care. Urgency should not, however, cause a permanent departure from a thoughtful approach. If a step such as hospitalization was not planned, then, once it has taken place, the goals of the risk plan need to be revised. The decision to hospitalize and its implications for other strategies have to be taken into account so that planned risk management and risk assessment can be resumed.

Where that degree of imminence is not at issue, then overall goals will be achieved through a series of smaller steps, planned in advance, taking into account practicalities, as well as substantive considerations about risk reduction. If possible, the subject of plans should be actively engaged in the process of setting out steps for change. In a study of looked-after children, Thomas (2011) found that they had not helped to write their care plan and, as a result, felt that they weren't listened to. While individuals may see the desirability of achieving long-term goals, sustaining motivation in the light of real-life difficulties and pressures requires the establishment of smaller achievable steps. We have already discussed the place of approach goals. Steps towards achieving these goals should be planned and service users helped to understand and contribute to how those steps fit together. In the case of Kay and Marcia mentioned earlier, an area of concern is the poor physical and psychological care provided for the child. The goal (framed as an approach goal) that Kay might be working towards could be 'At the end of three months, sit down with Marcia and together make a list of what has improved for her at home.' Steps to help mother and child achieve this are planned with them. A 'means–end thinking' approach, as illustrated in the activity below, can be used to plan for sequences of interventions. It encourages practitioners to be clear about the areas of risk they address and to define positive and specific outcomes in a particular time frame, before planning a sequence of steps to achieve those outcomes.

### Activity 4.8  'Means–End Thinking'

The table below can be used to plan a sequence of steps in a case. It could be used in the workplace or on placement. In the table, the first column has been completed in relation to Kay and Marcia as an illustration. You should then use this means–end approach to plan for a case with which you are involved, or to plan other areas of concern in Kay and Marcia's case. Follow these steps to complete the table.

- Identify key areas of concern, ideally agreed between the practitioner and the service user(s). Write each concern at the top of a column.
- Go to the bottom of each column and, for each area of concern, write the outcome you and the service user have agreed to work towards. Those outcomes should be framed where possible as approach goals and should be outcomes that support strengths as well as reduce risk.
- When each specific outcome is clear, list the particular interventions/ steps that can best achieve each in the order in which they should be completed.

**Means–End Thinking**

| Areas of concern you are addressing | Area of concern 1<br>Kay has not been providing clear parental support and guidance. This is creating risks for Marcia physically, developmentally and at school. | Area of concern 2, etc. |
|---|---|---|
| What steps need to be taken to achieve the desired outcome in each case? | Two sessions with Kay and Marcia to make a list of positive behaviours that Marcia should adopt and to clarify behaviours she should be avoiding. | |
| | Kay and Marcia should be helped to design and make a chart of positive behaviours. Chart to be used every day. | |

| | | |
|---|---|---|
| | Kay to have one-to-one skills sessions to help her improve her assertiveness and her ability to tackle problem behaviours clearly. | |
| | Kay to practise those skills. Both Kay and Marcia to have one or more sessions on their own to talk about how this is going and to rehearse their behaviours. | |
| What outcome are you and the service user hoping to achieve for each of the areas being considered? | At the end of two months, Kay will be able to tell Marcia 'well done' regularly and will be able to stick to practical boundaries. | |

You might also want to link the steps above to parallel work being done by others, for example in the case above work being done in school with Marcia. In reality, such plans also need to have a degree of flexibility. If an unexpected opportunity for positive change arises, a quick decision might need to be made to move in a different direction in order to make the most of this opportunity. If the steps do not take you in the desired direction, you may have to revisit the plan and add or remove some elements.

You will also have to think about how achieving one outcome successfully may depend on the prior achievement of another. In addition, the same interventions may also be relevant to more than one outcome. What other considerations should be taken into account?

- To achieve a desired outcome, you may need to include some restrictive interventions to ensure that ongoing work can be delivered with sufficient safety.

- Resource considerations will make a difference to planning. For example, if a particular residential placement is not immediately available, then interim plans will need to be made.
- The likelihood of the success of an intervention must be considered. In an ideal world an intervention designed to reduce substance misuse may seem most important, but, if the level of motivation is low, it may be unrealistic and another more achievable step might need to come first. Including positive strengths-based goals can be important for supporting motivation.
- There will be difficult choices to be made. If a person with a learning difficulty is to be able to live independently with reasonable safety, he/she may need to be given help to acquire the relevant skills. If, however, some of those skills can only really be learnt in a more independent setting, then there may be difficult questions of timing to answer in order to inform the decision about when a move to independence should take place. Risk taking may be an important part of the plan.
- What timescales are you working within? For older people, contact with agencies is often quite short-lived and at a time of crisis (Bornat and Bytheway 2010). It may be necessary to take speedy action to prevent the likelihood of much greater deterioration in the relatively near future, but this action may stabilize the situation and reduce risk without the need for further intervention. There is of course a dilemma about when services should be delivered. It is arguable that more effective preventative interventions at an earlier stage would avoid the need for more intrusive intervention once risk has escalated. Children's lives run on different timetables to those of adults. Preventing long-term harm to children and young people as they grow up may require incisive decision making at a young age; witness the developing public debate about the extent and timeliness of adoption. (Department for Education 2011)

All of this complexity has to make sense to the service users who need help to see a path through to achievable goals. The means–end approach above can help to explain planning to them, as can the suggestion in the activity below.

---

**Activity 4.9   Footsteps to Change**

One method which has been used very helpfully with young people and their families is the analogy of 'footsteps' to change (Callaghan, Kelly and Wilkinson 2009). The steps planned for in the means–end approach above can be developed and used more interactively with service users.

- Cut out foot shapes from cardboard.
- With the young person, and possibly their family, identify a goal, and work out the actions that will need to be taken to achieve that goal.
- Write each action on individual foot shapes and lay them out. They can include actions to be taken by children, by their parents and of course by the worker.
- Together agree the order in which these steps to change need to occur.
- How might you use or adapt this approach for shared planning with service users with whom you work? Do you have other approaches which achieve a similar result?

---

## Contingency Planning

No matter how carefully a plan has been put together, the uncertainties of life mean that unforeseen outcomes will occur. Paradoxically, a planned approach can make flexibility more achievable so that practitioners can respond appropriately to unexpected developments. If the plan has clear outcomes and strategies, then it can be adapted to meet changing situations, while retaining its clarity of purpose. Difficulties that might arise can of course to some extent be anticipated. Another strand of planning involves looking ahead to possible difficulties so that alternative actions which meet a range of contingencies can be built in from the outset.

Risk, as well as being uncertain, is likely to change over time. A risk manager needs to know what factors are most likely to signal escalating risk and growing imminence. Just as with general risk factors, it is possible to identify common elements that often mean that risk may be increasing. For example, some general factors include:

- changes in compliance with services;
- increasing substance misuse;
- a breakdown in support;
- the loss of accommodation or employment;

- relationship breakdown. (Kemshall, Mackenzie, Miller and Wilkinson 2011)

However, the practitioner also needs to be knowledgeable about the individual case, in particular the specific risk factors and triggers for harmful behaviour that have been identified as significant.

Chapter 3 considered the biases in thinking that can make a risk assessor less likely to recognize the importance of changing information. It raised the idea of looking at a range of outcomes and scenarios and thinking ahead about possibilities. Scenario planning can be used to put in place plans that take into account a range of possibilities (RMA 2007; Kemshall, Mackenzie, Miller and Wilkinson 2011). It asks you to consider possible future scenarios in order to plan actively for a range of potential outcomes. Scenarios are not suggested because they *will* happen but because they *may*; they are outlined in order to help identify proportional protective measures that can be taken from the outset and to put in place contingency plans should a harmful incident become more likely or imminent. Scenario planning is intended to help practitioners avoid the false assumption that future behaviours and situations will be identical to those they are faced with in the present.

It can be very helpful to take some time to think about what might change. Consider, for example, a situation where a child has been injured by a partner of the main carer (the mother); the man has now left the family. Clear decisions may already have been taken about what steps will be necessary if he returns. What if a new partner comes onto the scene? Scenario planning would ask the practitioner to think in some detail about a range of possibilities and to take those into account in current planning, for example in deciding what work needs to be done with the mother to help her think through realistically how she should make future decisions so that the safety of her children remains paramount. Contingency plans could also be put into place for this potential new situation.

---

### Activity 4.10   Scenario Planning

**Scenario planning 1**
More detailed scenario planning for a case can be completed using the framework below. This would be useful, for example, as part of ongoing supervision of an experienced practitioner and as an activity on, or in preparation for, a placement:

- Based on knowledge of the case, what has happened in the past?
- Drawing on a number of past behaviours and situations, identify a range of possible changes that might happen, both individual and situational.
- Having identified some possible changes, generate scenarios that incorporate each of the changes in turn. What might happen? Think about the potential for escalation in likelihood, imminence, or extent of harm.
- Discount scenarios that are too alike and any that are just not believable. From the remainder, see if it is possible to identify any new triggers, risk factors or protective factors.
- Use the elements identified to check if any amendments are needed to the existing plan and put into place appropriate proportional contingency plans if needed.

A forward-looking approach to planning is also relevant for making the most of positive future developments. A new family member may not always pose a risk; they may bring with them the potential for positive support and help. Balanced contingency planning will weigh up both positive and negative factors.

**Activity 4.11 Remembering the Potential for Positive Change**

Scenario planning 2
Return to the scenario planning activity above.

- Has the process included sufficiently potential positive changes?
- Do the contingency plans allow the practitioner to make the most of those changes?

## Recording, Monitoring and Review

The next chapter considers the review and quality management of risk practice in more detail. Where possible review, like planning, should be participative, with service users actively engaged in reviewing progress towards desired outcomes. Review also has to look at the processes that have taken place. Have they been delivered as planned? Have the standards of defensible practice been met? Review will depend in part on the quality and relevance of the recording that has taken place.

Figure 1.1 was specific about the importance of recording not only during assessment but also during ongoing intervention. The plans put in place need to be recorded, shared and agreed with the subject of the intervention. The details and impact of interventions should also be recorded, along with other significant changes or new information. Both the processes that have taken place and the outcomes that have resulted should be recorded.

There is a tension between time spent with families or individuals and time spent recording information. Recording, like risk intervention, should be proportionate but records do matter because they help to:

- maintain continuity across workers and settings;
- evidence the basis for often difficult and finely balanced decisions;
- demonstrate the work that has been done;
- evidence the impact of the work on specific outcomes and the overall goal of risk reduction;
- support analysis and planning;
- allow individuals and agencies to demonstrate defensible practice.

Don't forget that ongoing risk assessments often depend on the identification of patterns over time, so the recording of precise accounts can be essential (Munro 2008a).

The website www.writeenough.org.uk contains a wealth of activities and support for effective recording. It identifies the following pitfalls for practitioners:

- case records are out of date;
- the child is 'missing' from the record;
- facts and professional judgements are not distinguished in the record;
- the size of the record makes it difficult to manage;
- there is no assessment on file;
- the record is not written for sharing;
- the record is not used as a tool for analysis;
- the record is disrespectful to the service user.

Records are potentially powerful. Once something is written down, it gains authority and can appear fixed. Judgements separated from their evidence can come to be seen as facts which remain with service users over time (Milner and O'Byrne 2009). On the other hand, careful recording of decision making can help to safeguard the rights of the assessed by making the basis of judgements explicit (McDonald 2010b). Hall and Slembrouck (2009) describe recording as a strategic action, not simply reporting information. When recording a case, practitioners make choices about what to emphasize and those choices influence how other people then perceive and understand their actions.

However, the record needs to be actively used. Ongoing information gathering, monitoring and the recording of new information and changes over time may contribute to changing views of risk. On a regular and ongoing basis, practitioners should also reflect on the steps that are being taken and the effect on outcomes. This review should also regularly involve service users and others involved in the case. Plans should sometimes be modified in the light of experience, usually by making small-scale changes but sometimes necessitating a rethink of the plan as a whole.

---

### Activity 4.12   Reading Case Records

It is very interesting to look at a case record in some detail and ask does it:

- help the reader understand both the process and content of the work that has been undertaken?
- help the reader understand the risk factors being addressed and how interventions have affected outcomes?
- clearly signpost changes and the steps taken to address them?
- show that the service users have played an active and ongoing part in planning and review?
- demonstrate a balance between maintaining a clear outcome-focused plan and being responsive to change?

---

## Skills in Working with Others

Effective risk management almost always requires working with others, both within a particular agency and in inter-agency contexts. Those relationships can be productive and make a real difference, but in practice they are sometimes problematic and at worst such relationships can play a part in failures to manage risk effectively (Brandon et al. 2008a). Difficulties between agencies can affect involvement at an early stage, with, for example, the failure by other agencies to report information, affecting decisions around thresholds (Appleton and Oates 2010).

It is important to seek to understand the systemic reasons why effective working relationships are not always achieved. The way in which differences in categorization can affect working together was raised earlier (Hall and Slembrouck 2009). This suggests that once a case is ascribed an agency category, professionals will tend to interpret all new information in the light of that categorization. If the relative of an older person is categorized as over-anxious and demanding, important information they have to offer about risk may be discounted. They are even more likely to be categorized in that way by practitioners struggling with limited resources.

How professionals in different agencies conceptualize their roles and the decisions they need to make may affect working together. In a study of an organization working with homeless women, Juhila (2009) identified 'interpretive repertoires' used by workers in practice. Such repertoires can shape and influence practitioners' approaches to practice. She observed a range of interpretations, including caring, assessment, control, therapy, service provision and fellowship. Taylor (2006) similarly discusses what he describes as risk-management paradigms, which are influential in making decisions about the long-time care of older people. He suggests that health and social services professionals responded to uncertain situations by using a number of distinct paradigms, alongside their own assumptions. For example, some used a paradigm of accounting for resources and priorities, others a paradigm of identifying and meeting needs. While these paradigms share a present rather than future-oriented perspective, the first may be more driven by urgency, whereas the second more by the views and wishes of an individual or family. If such different paradigms are operating in an unspoken way in a risk-planning meeting, for example, very different courses of action might be advocated, without those concerned fully understanding what their differences of opinion are about. In inter-professional communication, practitioners need to clarify the meaning they have ascribed to the facts and be careful to distinguish between inferences and observations.

Meetings and discussions should also be purposeful. Otherwise they become ends in themselves, with safe practice being seen as having held the meeting rather than 'whether intelligent discussion took place' (Munro 2008b). It has also been suggested that decision making in groups can give the illusion of fairness and objectivity, but groups, like individuals, are still prone to bias and error. For example, groups are more likely to reach agreement around a high- or low-risk assessment than a moderate one (Munro 2008a). Groups can find it difficult to manage conflicting views and this may produce pressure towards conformity. Nash (2010) suggests that, if one categorization or way of seeing things dominates, there are dangers that multi-agency working can lead to a single mono-agency view of a problem.

---

**Activity 4.13    Agency and Practitioner Perspectives in Risk Meetings**

Rather than just attending risk meetings and taking the way in which they operate for granted, it is useful to reflect on the processes that have operated for good or ill. The following questions can be used to review a meeting you have attended that was concerned with risk and that included a number of agency and/or professional perspectives. It could also be used to review a recording that has been made of a meeting if those involved are in agreement:

*   Did the meeting keep a clear focus on its stated purpose(s)?
*   How successfully did the discussion strike a balance between enabling participants to put their own perspectives and encouraging openness to the perspectives of others?
*   Did particular viewpoint(s) dominate and, if so, what effect did this have?
*   What interpretive repertoires or paradigms could you identify amongst the participants in the discussion? What effect did they have?
*   If there were a number of plans for a client, was relevant attention paid to ensuring that they all worked together and did not conflict?

If you are participating in meetings about risk, keep these questions in mind. They may help you steer the discussion in more useful ways.

---

## Conclusion

This chapter has emphasized the importance of a structured, planned but flexible approach to risk-management planning and the subsequent delivery, review and recording of the work undertaken. Plans must explain how risk management has been derived from the risk assessment, what outcomes are being sought and what strategies are being used to achieve those outcomes. Outcomes should address risk reduction and positive outcomes for service users. Strategies must allow for appropriate risk taking, as well as risk reduction, and where possible contingency planning should be built in from the outset.

Key stages in planning and delivering risk management have been identified and worked through and the importance of working with others highlighted. Working with others also includes a participative and collaborative approach to the ongoing working relationship with service users as fully as possible in the interests of retaining a clear focus on risk reduction.

## Further Reading

Darlington, Y., Healy, K. and Feeney, J. (2010) 'Challenges in implementing participatory practice in child protection: a contingency approach', www.sciencedirect.com/science/article/pii/S0190740910001039, accessed 3 March 2013.

Maden, T. (2011) 'Mental health and risk', in H. Kemshall and B. Wilkinson (eds), *Good Practice in Assessing Risk: Current Knowledge, Issues and Approaches*. London: Jessica Kingsley.

Munro, E. (2008) *Effective Child Protection*, 2nd edn. London: Sage.

# 5

# Risk and Ethics

Ethics is defined as 'the science of morals in human conduct' (*Oxford English Dictionary* 2010) and it has been seen as critical to the practice of social work since the early twentieth century (Barry 2009). Social work is a profession grounded in the lives of people, their social contexts, rights, choices, issues and problems. As such, it can present tensions between 'social control, social care, social justice and social change' (Barry 2009: 111). In a recent consultation exercise, the British Association of Social Workers (BASW 2012a) found that the most common ethical dilemmas faced by practitioners were: care versus control issues, conflicting rights, for example between child and parents, compulsory detention of persons with a mental disorder and adult protection from self-harm versus rights and choices. In its code of ethics, the BASW summed this up as:

Ethical problems often arise because social workers:

- work with conflicting interests and competing rights;
- have a role to support, protect and empower people, as well as having statutory duties and other obligations that may be coercive and restrict people's freedoms;
- are constrained by the availability of resources and institutional policies in society. (BASW 2012b: 6)

Professional standards and codes of ethics are often used to resolve such tensions, enabling practitioners to balance the risks, rights and needs of users and the often contradictory needs and rights of users and those people affected by them. Social work is therefore a profession characterized by ethical challenges and dilemmas (Dolgoff, Harrington and Loewenberg 2011). Such dilemmas can be understood as differing or difficult choices, sometimes including choices where there is no possibility of a good outcome; or choices that are constrained in some way, for example by a lack of resources. As Titterton puts it: 'A welfare dilemma involves choices that welfare professionals, vulnerable people, their informal carers and their commitments face between options that entail possible benefits and possible harms. These choices may be equally acceptable but their outcomes essentially remain unknown' (2005: 50). He goes on to remind us that there is no such thing as a 'risk-free option', but rather degrees of risk and acceptability.

Workers find such decisions troublesome and troubling. These decisions are most apparent when:

- the social work role and responsibilities conflict with a worker's own ethical beliefs and values;
- service-user rights and choices are potentially or actually constrained by the actions the worker proposes to take. Sometimes this is to protect others; sometimes it is to protect the service user. This is sometimes expressed as a clash between risks and rights;
- a situation has no clear-cut answer, or where a number of options/responses are unlikely to achieve good outcomes (the worker may experience this in terms of the 'least bad option'), or where the best option cannot be resourced and workers may feel they are obliged to persuade service users to 'make do' with inadequate services;
- role boundaries are compromised or threatened. Workers may collude or 'befriend' service users. This is particularly acute if the service user is vulnerable. Workers may occupy dual roles, for example to support carers and also to act in the best interests of the individual service user (the 'cared for'). This can produce conflicts and ethical dilemmas about 'what to do for the best' and tensions about whose 'best interests' the worker is there to ensure.

Considering ethical dilemmas also raises issues about personal integrity and professional conduct, particularly in the operation of role boundaries and the requirement to act in 'a reliable, honest and trustworthy manner' (BASW 2010b: 10). We will review these key ethical issues and provide a practice framework for tackling them. This is a complex and challenging area of work and this chapter does not claim to have all the answers! However, it will equip you to consider and weigh up ethical dilemmas in a more robust and rigorous way. As Dolgoff, Harrington and Loewenberg put it, we should be less focused on presenting solutions and encourage workers to: '(a) be alert to discovering and perceiving ethical issues; (b) be clearer about the values that affect their decision making; (c) consider competing arguments, in examining both the strengths and limitations of their own positions, and in reaching thoughtfully reasoned conclusions' (2011: x).

Banks (2011) refers to an 'ethics boom' evidenced by a growth in literature and guidance over the last decade. She argues that the definitions and focus on ethics in northern and western countries have been about the development of principles to regulate conduct, to assist practitioners to make difficult choices and to support service users to make their own choices. Both guidance and literature tend to address 'ethical theories, codes of ethics, practice-related dilemmas and ethical decision making' (Banks 2011: 8; 2012). Ethical codes produced by professional bodies (e.g. the BASW 2012b) tend to have a practical focus and provide not only core values to underpin the code, but also standards and rules of operation. Ethical codes have become more standardized and prescriptive (Banks 2011, 2012), and those rooted in western perspectives of individualism and human rights have been critiqued on the grounds that they do not necessarily apply to non-western countries. This is an extensive debate in which the claim to universalism of some ethical codes (e.g. the International Federation of Social Workers (IFSW) code of ethics; see end of chapter for website details) has been increasingly challenged. This chapter does not engage with that debate but focuses on the types of ethical dilemmas and practice codes prevalent in anglophone countries (for a review of the debate, see Banks 2011; see also Gilbert 2009). The emphasis in this chapter will be on critical reflection and weighing options when considering solutions to the ethical dilemmas of daily practice.

## Role, Responsibilities and Ethical Beliefs

Social work is a value-laden profession. Workers bring values with them into the workplace, many of which are both desirable and sought, for example value commitments to diversity and equality. However, the worker's value base is expected to be compatible with the aims and objectives of employing agencies and should be deployed with reasonable care and consideration. As Reamer has argued (1983, 2006), this can lead to conflicts between a practitioner's obligations both to the service user and to their employer, and this can be particularly acute where the service user is compelled to use the service.

For example, most probation officers and criminal justice social workers will have a belief and commitment to the rehabilitation of offenders, and will have chosen their profession and been recruited with that value belief in mind. However, this commitment to rehabilitation has to be balanced against the risks posed by the offender to victims and the wider public (Kemshall 2008c), and both the employing agency and the public would expect workers to be able to properly weigh up such decisions. Consider the following case study and the ethical dilemmas posed by policy and legislation in this instance:

---

### Activity 5.1   Case Study

On 9 July 1996 Lin Russell and her two daughters, Megan and Josie, aged six and nine respectively, were walking down a Kent country lane when they and their dog were viciously attacked. Lin and Megan died, Josie was severely injured and left for dead. The incident gave rise to instant and justifiable national horror (Francis 2006: 4).

Michael Stone was arrested one year after these murders were committed and was convicted of them in October 1998.

> Michael Stone is one of the group of patients who are among the most difficult and challenging for the health, social and probation services to deal with. He presented with a combination of problems: a severe antisocial personality disorder, multiple drug and alcohol abuse, and occasionally, psychotic symptoms consistent with the adverse effects of drug misuse and/or aspects of his personality disorder. This complex and shifting picture made consistent and accurate diagnosis difficult. (Francis 2006: 4)

**Commentary**

As part of its response to these events, the government announced its wish to introduce a new policy of preventive detention. This was based upon the concept of dangerous and severe personality disorder (DSPD). The policy would have meant permitting the detention of those such as Michael Stone, who may have met the DSPD criteria, before they had the opportunity to commit a serious offence. The government proposals rested upon according DSPD the status of a pseudo-diagnosis that could be determined using clinical assessment processes. These proposals were detailed in a Green Paper entitled 'Managing Dangerous and Severe Personality Disorder – Proposals for Policy Development', published in 1999. (Home Office and Department of Health 1999).

**Questions for reflection**

1   What ethical principles underpin the debate concerning the legitimacy of the proposals for preventive detention contained within the Green Paper referred to above?
2   In assessing and managing risk, how would you seek to strike the balance between public safety and individual liberty?

What importance do you attach to questions concerning the reliability of the process used to diagnose DSPD? (Lawrence Nuttall, Department of Social Work, University of West of Scotland, adapted from Francis 2006; reproduced with permission)

This case and subsequent debate over legislation provides an interesting snapshot of the tension between risks and rights. In this case, the tension was between the rights of potential DSPD persons to liberty and not to be detained in advance of committing any crime, the risks they present to the public from their at times unpredictable behaviour and the rights of the public to safety from possible serious harm. The impact of such legislation upon practitioners can be significant. They find themselves having to carry out risk assessments which can lead to detention and the infringement of rights, or if they fail to prevent a harmful crime, they can be blamed for failing to protect the public. The scenario also illustrates the pitfalls of deciding legislation and policy on infrequent, exceptional cases and in the absence of firm evidence. For example, Nuttall offers the following feedback commentary on the case study.

---

### Commentary on case study

The key argument used to support the DSPD proposals was that the threat to public safety posed by a small number of individuals who met the DSPD criteria was so grave that urgent action was required. The proposals were predicated on the assumption that preventive detention should be used, where possible, prior to any criminal offence having been committed. Critics of these proposals argued that DSPD represented a spurious diagnosis that was not rooted in evidence; furthermore, the DSPD proposals represented an attempt to misuse psychiatry for political purposes. Critics further argued that the policy was based on an inaccurate view of the reliability of predicting the specific occurrence of harmful events. One consequence of this would be that to successfully prevent one homicide being perpetrated by someone who met the DSPD criteria, 'six people with DSPD would need to be detained in order to prevent one person from acting violently' (Farnham and James 2001). The government argued, however, that these proposals were necessary because psychiatry as a profession had failed to live up to its responsibilities for working with those who would meet the DSPD criteria on the basis that they were generally considered to be untreatable: the then Home Secretary Jack Straw cited the case of Michael Stone as an example of this (Straw 1998). The debate concerning DSPD and preventive detention centres more broadly on the proper role and remit of medicine and more specifically on that of psychiatry. This debate is in turn framed within an even broader one about how the imperatives of public protection and the safeguarding of individual liberty should be balanced by governments and those responsible for assessing and managing risk. (Kindly provided by L. Nuttall, Department of Social Work, University of the West of Scotland)

---

The case study also illustrates that professional values and personal ethical beliefs can be at odds with the role and responsibility of the employing agency. For example, a worker may believe firmly in the maxim 'innocent until proved guilty', and consider the use of preventive detention as morally wrong and abhorrent. In these circumstances, working within an agency that takes on responsibilities of risk assessment to aid preventive detention may become untenable. As Reamer states, it is not unusual for social workers to experience ethical and value dilemmas between acting in the service user's best interest and obeying a law, policy or formal procedure (Reamer 1983; Barry 2009).

## *Managing 'threats' to my ethical beliefs*

Fortunately, most tensions between role, responsibility and ethical beliefs are less extreme, although nonetheless challenging. In social work with older persons, for example, workers may hold personal commitments to autonomy and the right to make choices. These may be tested by particular cases. For example, Stevenson (1999) argues that the desire to protect can quickly overtake commitments to autonomy, particularly if the judgement is that the older person is at risk of significant harm. The primary objective of the social work agency, and potentially the worker, can be to minimize the risk of significant harm (Titterton 2005: 53). This can be particularly acute if the employing agency is seeking to avoid blame, litigation or challenge. In these circumstances, workers can feel pressured, particularly by carers, family members and neighbours all demanding that 'something is done'. Similar difficulties occur in work with vulnerable adults where Preston-Shoot (2001) notes tensions between protection, self-determination, paternalism and autonomy (Titterton 2005: 54). As such challenges are a common factor of working life in social work, it is important that workers know their own ethical beliefs, how these might be challenged and how to respond to such challenges.

---

**Activity 5.2   My Own Ethical Beliefs**

Consider your own ethical beliefs.

- What core ethical beliefs do you hold?
- What beliefs influenced you to consider social work as a career?
- Have you experienced any challenges to your ethical beliefs from either student placements or your employment? What were these and how did you manage these challenges?
- What have you learnt from this exercise that will help you manage challenges to your ethical beliefs in your current or future employment?

---

During the exercise, you may have realized that the beliefs that brought you into the profession are often those that can be most challenged and compromised. Situations faced by workers are rarely clear-cut, but are often complex and involve numerous participants and stakeholders as well as service users. Workers can find themselves having to manage differing expectations and demands from a range of people, in situations characterized by degrees of risk and uncertainty. Titterton offers helpful guidance in navigating the types of challenges and welfare dilemmas that can arise from professional responsibility to assess and manage risk. He encourages workers to be explicit when considering options and choices and offers a framework for aiding workers to do this. This includes considering:

- the advantages and disadvantages of any option/choice for all parties involved (including the employing agency);
- clear calculations of risks and benefits;
- clear consideration of 'trade-offs', compromises, and likely desirable outcomes;
- explicit accounts of assumptions about what are (un)acceptable risks and for whom;
- the human rights that apply in the case, and the extent to which they are affected, limited, constrained or upheld. (Adapted from Titterton 2005: 55–6)

In addition, it is also essential to know, and be explicit about, your own ethical beliefs and values as these will often frame your 'take' on situations and influence your assessment and management of risk. A worker rooted in a strongly autonomous position will see risk as more acceptable than a worker rooted in a protectionist perspective – the latter will seek to minimize risks as much as possible. As Titterton puts it, balance between risk and safety is the important thing, along with a rigorous and explicit approach to achieving such a balance. The following questions can help us rigorously focus on ethical issues:

- How can the service user be included in risk-assessment and risk-management planning?
- What risks is the service user exposed to?
- What are the views of others in this case, and what rights do they have (if any)?
- How can risk reduction be balanced with quality of life, independence and the service user's own wishes?
- Which risks are acceptable? And which risks need to be mitigated?
- Are there any protective factors or support networks that can be used?

- Seek in every case to balance risk management with the service user's right to autonomy.

These questions could be used to explore more explicitly and robustly the ethical dilemmas in the case of Freda presented in chapter 3. You may wish to return to this case study and apply these questions now.

Balance is critical to assessment and management in cases of this type, and, as Titterton states, using a clear framework is essential to how such a balance is achieved (see p. 108 above). It is always desirable to balance the reduction of risk with the likely impact on quality of life, level of autonomy and independence. Risk-management strategies should be informed by the desire to balance risk reduction with autonomy, quality of life, human rights and human dignity (Kemshall 2002a: 125; see also Tindall 1997 for risk management of users with learning disabilities). These issues are further explored in the next section with particular reference to those service users who are compelled to receive a service/intervention.

## Service-User Rights and Choices, and the Management of Risk

Social workers can also be involved in *withdrawing* services, or at times *imposing* services and interventions, against the wishes of the service user (Shardlow 2002; Barry 2009). Services may be withdrawn because the worker perceives they are no longer of benefit to the user, but also because of scarce resources and differing priorities. Imposition of services can occur in compulsory settings like probation or mental health, but also in instances where workers believe a user may harm her/himself or others. Tensions can exist between service-user rights and choices, and worker responsibilities to manage risk, especially in situations where the most desirable options may not exist or cannot be funded. Important considerations when seeking to balance risks and rights are:

- What is the evidence that the risk is likely, and how significant will the harm be if the risk occurs?
- Who might be affected by this risk, how and to what extent?
- What strategies can be used to minimize the likelihood of the risk and its impact? List these strategies.

And then:

- Consider how each of these strategies affects the rights of the service user.
- Which strategy can provide optimal risk reduction with the least impact on rights? Can this strategy be funded and provided?
- Finally, how might your own ethical beliefs affect your decision making in this case? Is there anything you need to reconsider?

The BASW code of ethics attempts to reconcile the difficulty of balancing rights and risks thus:

> Social workers should recognize that people using social work services have the right to take risks and should enable them to identify and manage potential and actual risk, while seeking to ensure that their behaviour does not harm themselves or other people. Social workers should support people to reach informed decisions about their lives and promote their autonomy and independence, provided this does not conflict with their safety or with the rights of others. Social workers should only take actions which diminish people's civil or legal rights if it is ethically, professionally and legally justifiable. (BASW 2012b: 12)

In essence, workers should aim to protect and enhance the rights, choices and autonomy of service users unless 'required by law to protect that person or another from risk of serious harm' (BASW 2012b: 12).

The tension between rights and risks can be even more acute when the service user is under statutory supervision, for example in probation or criminal justice social work where the rights of the offender to privacy and to a 'fresh start' after a custodial sentence have to be weighed against the rights to protection, dignity and safety of potential or actual victims, and the rights of the wider public to be protected from harmful offenders. The general principle in the United Kingdom is that public and victim protection should outweigh offender rights, and that this is justified on the basis of a 'significant risk' of harm (Kemshall et al. 2011). Proportionality is, however, a key factor; intrusion and limits on rights cannot be excessive and must be proportionate to the actual risks presented. However, in the UK context, the state or agencies working on behalf of the state have an overriding duty to 'take suitable measures to protect the public'

(Department for Constitutional Affairs 2006: 35). It is important when you are trying to resolve the tension between risk and rights that you:

- know what the law allows and what the law expects you to do;
- remember that human rights do not necessarily 'trump' everything else. They have to be balanced against the rights of others and can be mitigated and limited by risks. It is important to be evidential and explicit, to weigh up and to balance;
- record your decision and the rationale for it clearly;
- use your professional standards as a framework to guide your decision. For example, the UK BASW code of ethics states:

Social workers should strive to carry out the stated aims of their employers or commissioners, provided they are consistent with the Code of Ethics. BASW expects employers to have in place systems and approaches to promote a climate which supports, monitors, reviews and takes the necessary action to ensure social workers can comply with the Code of Ethics and other requirements to deliver safe and effective practice. (BASW 2012b: 11)

## The Ethics of 'Making Do'

Social work takes place within particular economic and social contexts, and, in the post-2008 global crisis era, this inevitably means that social work services are constrained by the availability of resources. As one social worker has expressed it, 'the pressure to "turn over" a certain amount of cases versus your perspective of the time a case needs' (BASW 2012a) is a difficult ethical dilemma. Social workers are increasingly constrained by shrinking resources and the need to ration both access to and use of services by users. In essence, the dilemma is how to choose who gets what, and when to withdraw services if the cost outweighs the benefits. Contemporary social work practice is characterized by compromise and 'making do'. Rarely are we explicit as practitioners about our role as 'rationers'; nonetheless, it occurs and can engender negative emotions and ethical conflicts in daily practice (see also chapter 4 where thresholds of risk are discussed).

Consider the following activity.

---

### Activity 5.3   The Challenges of Rationing

This exercise can be done using a current case from your workload, a case from a student placement, or a case study provided to students by your social work course tutor.

Take a recent case where you had to provide a less than adequate service or withdraw support earlier than you wished.

- How did this decision make you feel and how did you manage your emotions?
- Why did you make this decision – what did you weigh up and consider when making it?

---

The activity will have highlighted that 'making do' and rationing resources is a perennial problem in social work practice. Decisions about priorities are routinely made, sometimes almost subconsciously, and it is common to feel pulled in different directions and experience negative emotions and dissatisfaction with service provision. This can be particularly acute when working with risk. Immediate and new risks can quickly overtake long-standing risk issues in a caseload, and it is easy for workers to turn their attention to new risks, allowing existing risks on their caseload to drift. Decisions about case priorities are not always explicitly made or reviewed, and practitioners may make these decisions without sufficient thought or reflection.

## Role Boundaries: Compromise and Collusion

Social workers are required to operate with personal and professional integrity. As the BASW's ethical code puts it: 'social workers have a responsibility to respect and uphold the values and principles of the profession and act in a reliable, honest and trustworthy manner' (2012b: 10). Central to this is the requirement to:

- uphold the values of the profession and avoid actions that would bring the profession into disrepute;

- be honest and trustworthy, including being honest and open about interventions, avoidance of manipulation and abuse of service users, employer or colleagues;
- maintain appropriate professional and role boundaries, and not abuse a position of trust for personal gain. (Adapted from BASW 2012b: 10)

Consider the following activity:

---

**Activity 5.4   Threats to Personal and Professional Integrity**

With a colleague/student, or perhaps in a small group of colleagues/students, use the following questions to lead discussion about potential threats to integrity. Use this to help you identify any ways in which these threats already are or could be minimized in your work or placement setting.

1   How might social workers manipulate service users?
2   Is it ever permissible to lie to a service user?
3   How might social workers abuse the trust of their employer?
4   How might social workers abuse their position of trust for personal gain?
5   How might role boundaries between social workers and service users be compromised?

---

The activity highlights that there are potentially numerous threats to personal and professional integrity. The profession can be brought into disrepute in various ways, and those mentioned here are not exhaustive. For example, social workers may (and have) leaked information on sensitive child-protection inquiries to the press. While 'whistle-blowing' on poor and unsafe practice is encouraged, there are particular procedures for this, and leaking confidential information for personal financial gain crosses role boundaries, breaks confidentiality codes and compromises professional integrity. Manipulation of service users is also possible. Workers and service users may form close relationships over the long term and in some instances service users may become dependent on such a relationship. Social workers may use a combination of power and trust to manipulate users into agreements and actions against their wishes or interests because it is in the social worker's interests – it reduces their workload, it is the least challenging option for them and so forth. Honesty, clarity and transparency with service users are important social work principles, and workers should operate on the basis that all their decisions are potentially open to scrutiny and challenge. Does this mean that social workers can never lie to service users? Interestingly, Barry (2009), following Reamer (1983), poses this question by using a specific example. A hospital social worker is asked by the family of a terminally ill patient not to tell the patient that they are dying. Should the social worker comply with this request? Let us consider this scenario:

---

**Activity 5.5   Can I Lie to You?**

A hospital social worker is asked by the family of a terminally ill patient not to tell the patient that they are dying. Should the social worker comply with this request?

1   Who is the client?
2   Whose rights, choices and autonomy is the social worker to uphold?
3   What considerations should the social worker take account of in coming to a decision?
4   Are there any circumstances in this scenario that may lead the social worker to lie? And would this be justified?

---

The client is the hospital patient and this person should be the social worker's primary concern, although it is easy to see how quickly the social worker could become compromised by pressure from family members with whom the worker may have sympathy and concern. However, the social worker has a primary duty to uphold the rights, choices and autonomy of the patient, but while working within the broader family network with a range of views, choices, needs and demands. A clear and consistent line with family members will be required. The social worker may wish to take into consideration the reasons and motivations of other family members in coming to their decision – these may provide important insights into family relationships or critical information about the patient's state of mind. Finally, could lying to the patient ever be justified? It may be difficult to accept but patients may subtly indicate that they do not actually want to learn that their condition is terminal, and workers may support that choice, or medical staff may indicate that knowing would worsen the patient's condition in the short term. It is important that workers act with clarity, are clear about their choices and that their decisions will withstand outside scrutiny. Adopting and holding appropriate role responsibilities and boundaries are critical in cases like this.

Leighton (1985) reminds us that social work relationships are professional and purposeful, and consequently are qualitatively different to personal ones. While it is important to form a relationship with service users, such relationships involve the use of power and authority and require the operation of suitable boundaries. The current BASW code of ethics states that: 'Social workers should establish appropriate boundaries in their relationships with service users and colleagues, and not abuse their position for personal benefit, financial gain, or sexual exploitation' (BASW 2012b: 10).

Regrettably, social workers can and have used their position of trust to put service users at risk of physical, sexual and emotional harms. One example is the case of Christopher Jarvis, a social worker employed by the Catholic Diocese of Plymouth to investigate child sexual abuse. He was later convicted of having 4,000 indecent images of young boys. Twelve of these were classed by police at level 5 which can include scenes of torture and sadism. In his job, Jarvis had access to confidential church files on at-risk children and signed off Criminal Records Bureau checks on other staff. Sentencing him, the judge said: 'Children who had confided in you may feel sullied and let down when they find out the person they were confiding in was downloading images in this way. You, of all people, were more aware than others of the massive theft of innocence and long-term damage exacted on the children whose images you downloaded for your own sexual gratification' (BBC News 2011).

Increasingly, the abuse of service users, particularly vulnerable children, by professionals is being recognized. The Home Education Forums website has literally 'put professional child abusers on the map'. In their words, 'To demonstrate just how many dangerous teachers, nursery staff, doctors, nurses, social workers, police officers, youth workers and other "caring" professionals there are out there, we have put a selection of state sanctioned professionals-turned-child abusers firmly *on the map*' (Home Education Forums, n.d.). Clicking on the words 'on the map' reveals a map of the United Kingdom showing the sites where professional abuse has taken place.

The most notorious case of recent times is that of the Little Teds nursery where Vanessa George abused toddlers and photographed her abuse, forwarding these pictures to others (BBC News 2010).

Interestingly, a review by the local safeguarding board found that the nursery was 'an ideal environment within which George could abuse'.

> While evidence pointed to George having no sexual interest in children until she came into contact with Blanchard [her male co-accused], it found there appeared to have been a complete lack of recognition of a culture in which explicit sexual references about adults in conversation were the norm.
>
> The review concluded that there was a "weak governance framework" at the private nursery with "no clear lines of accountability".
>
> It said the environment enabled a culture to develop in which staff did not feel able to challenge some inappropriate behaviour by George. (BBC News 2010)

Other staff at the nursery had become uncomfortable and concerned about George's behaviour but felt that they had nowhere to go and report it. A culture of silence prevailed, and this enabled George to continue her abuse.

While not all situations where social workers and other professionals put service users at risk are as extreme as these two cases, they do raise important issues for social workers. In particular, they highlight the role of scrutiny and challenge by colleagues, and the need to either make a direct challenge or report concerns to managers. Consider the following activity:

---

**Activity 5.6   Challenge and Reporting**

Use this exercise to reflect on things you have seen or heard during your student placements or employment as a social worker.

- Have you observed any behaviour by a colleague or fellow professional that made you feel uncomfortable?
- What was this behaviour and what do you think about it now?
- What do you need to do next time?
- What are the barriers to challenge and reporting in your team/agency?
- How can you get advice and support to 'do the right thing'?
- Find your agency's whistle-blowing procedure. How might this policy help you take action?

For an example of a whistle-blowing policy, see the BASW code at: www.basw.co.uk/resource/?id=770, accessed 3 March 2013.

---

Social workers may not directly and physically harm service users. However, their work with users may create dependency and erode autonomy, particularly where service users are perceived to be 'at risk'. This may present itself in a number of ways, for example:

- exercising high levels of influence over the service user's decision making;
- eroding the service user's right to make an informed choice;
- manipulating or exploiting the service user (e.g. financially);
- creating a level of dependency that erodes the user's future functioning as an independent person.

These responses to service users are often associated with overly restrictive risk-management approaches, focusing entirely on risk reduction with little attention to empowerment strategies (Titterton 2005). Risk management is not solely about risk elimination or even risk reduction. It is about balance, and may require the balancing of user wishes and aspirations with potential risks to the service user and others. As Titterton puts it: 'Risk management is more than simply risk minimization. It entails efforts to increase potential benefits and to provide a process for planning risk taking strategies and for monitoring and reviewing the results. Any risk management process must be both flexible and adaptable. A major challenge will be in promoting achievement-oriented visions of risk management' (2005: 93). Titterton argues that negotiation is critical to such situations. He cites Bibby's notion of 'assertive negotiation' which involves asserting our position while respecting the rights of others. Bibby (1994) offers the following as a helpful starting point (cited by Titterton 2005: 115):

- Ideal preferences should be stated.
- Do not negotiate the non-negotiable.
- Do not negotiate over positions.
- Prepare for give-and-take but know your boundaries.
- Know what you are trying to achieve.
- Separate people from the problem.
- Look at your interests and other people's interests.
- Be prepared to fail to agree.

Balance and negotiation are central to risk-management decisions about 'vulnerable' or at risk service users. The wishes and needs of the vulnerable person should be central, and, as Tindall argues, risk management should try to: 'maximise opportunities for people . . . to take risks which are carefully assessed and planned in order that they can maintain a good quality of life, develop new skills or try previously untried experiences' (Tindall 1997: 107). In this sense, risk management is transposed into carefully assessed and balanced risk taking.

Social workers can also find their position compromised, and their decision making impacted in various ways. The most obvious source of compromise is the loss of role boundary with service users, for example by establishing friendships or emotional relationships with users. Role confusion can also occur, with workers unclear about their role, what they are trying to achieve and the aims of their intervention with the service user. Workers can also find themselves manipulated by service users. For example, workers can be intimidated by service users, and fear and anxiety about risk issues can paralyse decision making. The role of 'Stockholm syndrome' in child protection failures has been known for some time (Goddard and Tucci 1991). In brief, the Stockholm syndrome refers to a psychological condition in which hostages bond with their captors out of fear, a syndrome named after the hostages taken at the Stockholm bank in 1973. On capture of the robbers and release of the hostages, the latter refused to testify against their captors and one was engaged to her captor. Goddard and Tucci apply this notion to child-abuse work, noting that much of the work is with 'involuntary clients', some of whom will be violent and threatening to the worker as well as to children. In essence, threat and implied threat, often from fathers or stepfathers, can prevent workers from visiting, asking pertinent questions when visiting, or thoroughly investigating what is happening to the child. Risk avoidance and risk aversion begin to permeate practice. This can happen in any working relationship where workers experience threat, fear and anxiety. Consider the following activity:

---

### Activity 5.7   Risk Avoidance and Risk Aversion

- In what situations are you most likely to engage in risk avoidance? Why?
- What tactics and strategies have you used to avoid risk or challenging situations?
- What strategies can you identify that would make you less likely to allow risk avoidance and aversion to impact on your decisions?

In these situations, objectivity and decision making are compromised.

## Summary and Conclusion

This chapter has reviewed some of the main ethical dilemmas facing practitioners. There are no easy answers but the chapter has attempted to offer a framework for considering such challenges, based on the work of Dolgoff, Harrington and Loewenberg (2011). In brief, these are:

- vigilance and alertness to ethical dilemmas;
- knowing oneself and the values which impinge on decision making;
- a robust mechanism for considering competing arguments, positions, needs and outcomes;
- the importance of clarity, reflection, transparency and rigour in 'reaching thoughtfully reasoned conclusions'. (Dolgoff, Harrington and Loewenberg 2011: x)

Ethical dilemmas are a fact of social work practice and must be positively approached rather than feared. This chapter has provided some basic tools to enhance confidence and enable a more explicit approach to ethical dilemmas. It is also important that practitioners refer to and actively use professional ethical codes. Again, these do not necessarily have all the answers to specific cases, but they do provide important underpinning principles and clear parameters within which decisions have to be made.

FURTHER READING

Banks, S. (2012) *Ethics and Values in Social Work*, 4th edn. BASW Macmillan Practical Social Work Series. Basingstoke: Palgrave Macmillan. Written by one of the leaders in the field of social work ethics, this provides new and interesting perspectives on the issue and is a 'must-read' for students and practitioners. Key definitions from this text form the basis of the BASW Code of Ethics.

British Association of Social Work (BASW) (2012) *The Code of Ethics for Social Work: Statement of Principles*. Available at: http://cdn.basw. co.uk/upload/basw_112315-7.pdf, accessed 27 February 2013. While a UK-based code, it does incorporate the International Ethics in Social Work – Statement of Principles (IFSW/IASSW rev. 2010). It provides a contemporary statement of professional standards and key values for social work practice. See also the BASW article entitled 'The Code Makers' explaining how the revised code of ethics was developed, available at: http://cdn.basw.co.uk/upload/basw_21546-9.pdf, accessed 27 February 2013.

Hothersall, S. and Maas-Lowitt, M. (2010) *Need, Risk and Protection in Social Work Practice*. Exeter: Learning Matters. This is a useful addition to the literature that focuses on practice issues and provides a good introduction to working with risk in social work and social care.

Hugman, R. (2005) *New Approaches in Ethics for the Caring Professions*. New York: Palgrave Macmillan. While a little dated, this text provides a useful overview of key issues and solutions for students. See also:

Hugman, R. (2008) 'An ethical perspective on social work', in M. Davies (ed.), *The Blackwell Companion to Social Work*, 3rd edn. Oxford: Blackwell.

For other ethical codes, see:

Australian Association of Social Workers (2010) *A Code of Ethics*. Canberra: Association of Social Workers. Available at: www.aasw.asn.au/document/item/740, accessed 27 February 2013.

National Association of Social Workers (2010) *A Code of Ethics*. Washington DC: NASW. Available at: www.puc.edu/__data/assets/pdf_file/0019/30097/NASW-Code-of-Ethics.pdf, accessed 27 February 2013.

The International Federation of Social Workers (IFSW) 'Statement of ethical principles'. Available at: http://ifsw.org/policies/code-of-ethics/, accessed 27 February 2013.

For a comparison of the International Code with the UK BASW code, see:

Gilbert, T. (2009) 'A comparison of the International Statement of Principles in Social Work with the Code of Ethics for British Social Workers', *The Journal of Social Work Values and Ethics* 6(2), available online at: www.socialworker.com/jswve/content/view/121/68/, accessed 27 February 2013.

# 6

# Review and Evaluation of Risk

Achieving high-quality risk-assessment and risk-management practice does not come easily or cheaply. It is the shared responsibility of practitioners and managers within an organization, requiring time, commitment and resources. Effective risk work needs to be identified, encouraged and shared; problematic practice needs to be tackled so that improvements can be made. Where there are clear failures in practice, there is a responsibility on all involved to learn from those mistakes.

As noted in previous chapters, the decisions and choices made by any individual worker are shaped by a range of practical, cultural and organizational factors (Calder 2008a, 2008b; Carson and Bain 2008; Wilson 2009; Bissell 2012). A systems perspective (Munro 2010a, 2010c) implies that there are shared personal and corporate responsibilities for developing practice. Individuals need to be active in reviewing their own work, but organizations also have an obligation to operate in a way that encourages and facilitates learning. Senge argues that '[a]n organization's commitment to and capacity for learning can be no greater than that of its members' (Senge 2006: 7). Individual practitioners need to take responsibility for learning and '[m]anagers should be actively striving to help their staff understand how good they are at risk decision-making, and how they might improve' (Carson and Bain 2008: 63). Effective risk practice within an organization therefore requires:

- risk policies and procedures that are fit for purpose;
- rigorous audit and quality assurance (QA) processes;

- mechanisms for communicating and discussing risk performance issues;
- a culture of improvement rather than blame;
- individuals and organizations taking and sharing responsibility;
- ongoing commitment to continuous learning and professional development.

The review and evaluation of risk practice can include a range of activities. For example, it may involve learning from an incident within your team, analysing monitoring data collected about routine practice over time or looking at the lessons learnt from a major public inquiry.

---

**Activity 6.1   Reflective Exercise on Opportunities for Learning**

This activity helps you to think about various different opportunities for learning about risk and improving practice. You may have come across some or all of the following during teaching and training, on placement, or in the workplace, as a manager or a practitioner.

1   A serious risk incident that you have been directly involved in.
2   Data from local performance monitoring.
3   Inquiries and reports relating to high-profile cases.
  - Have you had the opportunity to learn from any of the above? If so, what was helpful and what were the challenges?
  - For those sources you have not had direct experience of, what do you anticipate might be the challenges in learning from them?
  - What opportunities do you have now to learn from these sources?
  - How are you able to promote learning from them within your organization?

---

There can be difficulties associated with each of these. For example, direct involvement in a case can make it hard to be objective, whereas recommendations from public inquiries may not be easy to apply in a specific local context. This chapter will explore these and other approaches to reviewing risk practice. The aim is to demonstrate applications from the literature for both frontline practitioners and those in management roles to help show 'how local systems can become more reflective and adaptive learning organizations which instil a fair culture of transparency and accountability and how such an approach could secure the levels of improvement in practice that have not followed previous reforms' (Munro 2010c: 38). Some of the activities in this chapter are more appropriate for managers, but practitioners may also find them helpful as a prompt to reflect on aspects of organizational structure and the working environment.

## Learning from Inquiries and Serious Case Reviews

For each sphere of social work activity, there are procedures for instigating inquiries following serious incidents. In child protection, for example, the Working Together guidance (DCSF 2010) sets out the criteria for when a serious case review (SCR) is required. Since June 2010, all SCRs are now published (Loughton 2010) and notable examples have included the reports into the cases of Baby P, Khyra Ishaq and the 'J' children in Edlington (see http://education.gov.uk/ childrenandyoungpeople/safeguardingchildren/reviews). The rationale for making such information publicly available is that it will help to improve the dissemination of learning: '[t]he policy of publishing SCRs is intended to explain the many difficult decisions that have to be taken on a daily basis when working with vulnerable children' (Gove 2012: 2). For those working in mental health services, guidelines from the Department of Health specify when inquiries are required and indicate that the investigation process and publication of reports 'should take place as soon as possible after the adverse event' (DoH 2005: 2).

When serious incidents occur – which they inevitably will in the complex world of social work – the inquiry process which follows can often be experienced by practitioners as a stressful process. This can add to the emotional strain of dealing with the incident itself and the fear of being blamed may be exacerbated by concerns about criticism from the media. An alternative view might be that inquiries are a bureaucratic process leading to long reports that don't seem to have much relation to real-life practice. In between these ends of the spectrum is the perhaps more common view that reports from inquiries are useful but there is often no time to absorb and apply the findings given the busy reality of the everyday working environment.

### Key lessons

In looking at the key lessons from serious incident inquiries, there is an extensive literature to draw on. Firstly, there are of course reports relating to specific cases (such as Ritchie, Dick and Lingham 1994; Blom-Cooper, Hally and Murphy 1995; Laming 2003). Secondly, there are reviews which highlight common themes emerging from a number of reports over time (such as Sheppard 1996; Prins 1999; Sinclair and Bullock 2002; Rose and Barnes 2008; Verita and Capsticks 2008; Brandon, Bailey and Belderson 2010). Thirdly, there are some insightful discussions comparing the issues raised by inquiries with issues raised in academic papers (see, for example, Calder 2011: 198–200).

Some of the recurring areas of concern identified in the reports – which apply across the different spheres of social work – are summarized below.

*Communication between professionals* Poor communication between professionals is often identified in reports as an 'area of weakness' (Stanley and Manthorpe 2001: 85). This can be caused by a range of factors, such as: reluctance to share information based on the mistaken belief that 'knowledge equals power'; mistrust between organizations; or an inability to interpret information provided by others from a different professional background. These problems were seen in the case of Victoria Climbié with, for example, one doctor stating that 'I cannot account for the way other people interpreted what I said. It was not the way I would have liked it to have been interpreted' (Schwartz in Laming 2003: 9). The report into her death makes clear that '[e]ach agency must accept responsibility for making sure that information passed to another agency is clear, and the recipients should query any points of uncertainty' (Laming 2003: 9).

*Communication between professionals, service users and their families/carers* A recurring theme in mental health inquiries is that of poor communication between practitioners and non-professionals (spouses, siblings, other family members) closely involved in the client's life (Prins 1999). In the Andrew Robinson case, for example, the attempts by his parents to alert professionals to their concerns were repeatedly overlooked (Blom-Cooper, Hally and Murphy 1995). More surprisingly perhaps, but again a recurring problem, is a lack of communication between professionals and the primary service user. It was noted, for example, that very few professionals spent time talking to Victoria Climbié directly, even though opportunities were available (Laming 2003).

*Assessment* The challenges of assessment in social work practice are well documented (as discussed in chapters 2–4) and inquiries often highlight weaknesses in this area. There are too many issues to discuss in detail here but one example is that of social workers sometimes losing sight of who should be the main focus of attention, for example, focusing too much on the needs of a parent and not enough on those of the child (Rose and Barnes 2008). A second example of a common theme is the potential dangers of misinterpreting cooperation (or partial cooperation) by a client and allowing this to obscure an evaluation of the risks presented by particular circumstances or behaviours (Brandon et al. 2008a).

*Staff training and supervision* Lack of sufficient, high quality supervision is another common theme; for example in the case of Baby P, '[t]he case supervision, particularly for one of the social workers in Peter's case, was ad hoc, inconsistent, and often cancelled' (Haringey LSCB 2009: 24). An absence of supervision leads to a problematic lack of scrutiny of professional practice (Brandon et al. 2008a: 92). Chapter 7 looks at some of the practical questions of how to achieve a balanced effective approach to supervision. The importance of training is another topic frequently mentioned in inquiries (Reder and Duncan 2004b: 101), including the need for practitioners to have improved knowledge of inter-agency working (Laming 2003).

*Resources* Given the emotionally draining nature of social work, a lack of resources can have a significantly detrimental impact on practice. Reder and Duncan's comment on the Climbié case, that 'practitioners felt overwhelmed by the demands of their caseloads and demoralized by working in grossly underfunded and understaffed teams' (2004a: 111), could equally be applied to many other cases (see chapter 7 for a discussion of practical approaches to manage a stressful working environment). A shortage of resources can limit the time available to staff to develop relationships with clients, which in turn can lead to problems such as missing or misinterpreting significant information. The recurrence of this issue in inquiries has led to calls for restricted caseloads for key workers (Stanley and Manthorpe 2001: 92).

This is by no means a complete list and there are other recurring themes, such as poor quality record keeping, over-preoccupation with thresholds and lack of attention to or difficulties engaging with the cultural background of service users. The similarities in the findings from these inquiries over many years present something of a paradox. On the one hand, it seems clear that these reports can provide 'an invaluable source of teaching and learning material' (Balen and Masson 2008: 129). On the other hand, the fact that reports keep identifying similar problems suggests that this learning is not really happening in practice (Peay 1996; Reder and Duncan 2004b; Munro 2010c).

Why don't inquiries always have the impact on practice that might be expected? The style of inquiry reports has been noted as one factor that might limit their potential as tools for learning. For example, they can have a number of purposes – reassuring the public, protecting an organization's reputation by being seen to be 'doing something' – which means that they are not always written in ways that are the most useful for promoting learning (Cambridge 2004). Nevertheless, managers should ensure that staff have sight of reports and that opportunities are provided to reflect on how they might apply to local practice (Baker, Kelly and Wilkinson 2011).

## Report recommendations

Downham and Lingham (2009: 59–60) suggest that there are different types of recommendations that typically arise from serious incident reviews:

1   Practical: recommendations which may often be obvious and require straightforward practical implementation.
2   Commitment: recommendations framed in terms of commitment to a specific service improvement, for example to promote greater involvement of service users and carers.
3   Policy and procedural: recommendations which require writing *and* implementing revised operational policies or procedures.
4   Professional practice: recommendations that relate to the need for improvements in the standards of professional practice.
5   Major organizational change: some recommendations may require larger-scale change, either within an organization or in partnership arrangements with other organizations.
6   Commissioning: planning changes to service delivery or organizational ways of working may sometimes need to involve different commissioning bodies (e.g. local authorities and primary care trusts).
7   National: if a finding has national implications, the recommendations may feed into an existing research project or

consultation process. There may be an inquiry, extensive publicity and/or the involvement of experts in recommending solutions.

8  Common themes: these may be recorded in order to contribute to local or national reviews which aim to identify trends and recurring problems. These can often relate to the most difficult and intractable issues.

The different types of recommendations will vary in the amount of time and resources required for implementation. The list starts from recommendations which are focused on frontline practice and then moves outwards to wider policy and organizational issues. These may not be so directly related to everyday service delivery but can nevertheless be crucial to shaping the context and culture in which practice occurs. Not all reports will contain examples of each type of recommendation but most will contain a mixture.

---

**Activity 6.2  Responding to Recommendations**

It can be useful to think about these different types of recommendations by considering a specific case, and this is relevant to both practitioners and managers. If you have been directly involved in a serious case review, use that review as the example. If not, think about another serious case review or report that you have seen.

Identify examples of the different types of recommendations:

- Which do you think are most important/useful in this case?
- Are there any that you disagree with – why?
- If you have direct knowledge of this case, were the recommendations implemented? If not, what individual and organizational factors supported or prevented successful implementation?
- If you do not have direct knowledge, make a note of key individual and organizational factors that need to be in place for these recommendations to be successfully implemented.

---

A key conclusion from reviews of inquiries over the years is that improvements to routine practice will help to reduce the likelihood of serious incidents occurring. In their review of mental health inquiries, for example, McGrath and Oyebode state that '[t]he bulk of the recommendations suggest improvements to everyday tasks essential to providing a good mental health service' (2002: 65). Learning from inquiries should not therefore be seen as a separate or special activity that is only triggered by the occurrence of exceptional events but should be part of the ongoing process of practice improvement.

### *Changing practice: the impact of reviews and reports*

How does this process of practice improvement occur and what might be the obstacles that prevent it from happening? Sidebotham et al. (2010) usefully distinguish between the process of learning lessons at the local level (e.g. from a specific SCR) and from the broader analyses of SCRs. To begin at the local level, Figure 6.1 opposite illustrates two possible organizational responses to a serious incident review.

In the negative cycle, the service user is largely absent and the organizational response leads to a culture of fear and blame whereas, in the positive cycle, there is a much greater emphasis on an open approach to learning.

---

**Activity 6.3    Organizational Responses to Serious Incidents**

Responding appropriately to serious incidents can be a difficult and challenging task. If you have experience of working in an organization where a serious case/incident review has occurred, consider:

- Was the organization's response closer to the negative cycle or the positive cycle?
- Which factors most influenced the organization's approach?
- What were the benefits/disadvantages of the approach taken?

Now think about your own personal response and actions:

- How did you react?
- Were you in a positive or negative cycle?
- What more could you have done to react in a positive, constructive way?

If you have not yet had any personal involvement in serious incident reviews, think ahead to what you might do if it happens in future. What can you do now to develop your practice so that you can respond in a positive way to such reviews?

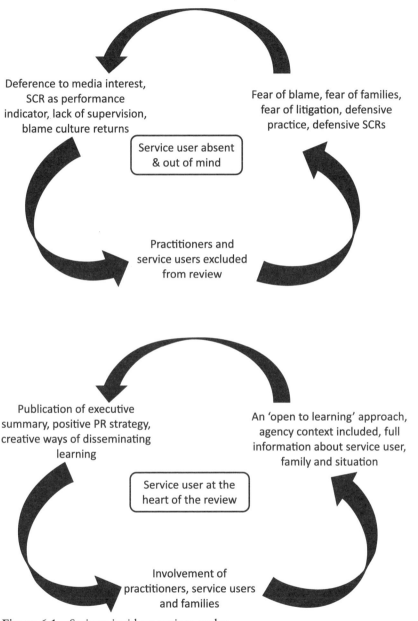

**Figure 6.1** Serious incident review cycles
*Source*: adapted from Brandon et al. 2009: 106.

Moving on to consider a wider regional or national perspective, there are (as noted above) numerous summaries which draw together the lessons emerging from different reports. Learning from these thematic analyses presents different challenges. There may be less of a problem with the defensiveness seen in the negative cycle reaction to SCRs discussed above, but more of a problem with taking the recommendations seriously at a local level. A summary which pulls together lessons from a variety of reports may seem remote from immediate practice in your particular organization and there might be a temptation to ignore it or downplay its significance.

---

### Activity 6.4   Learning from Recurring Problems

Read through a summary that pulls together lessons from a variety of reports. For example, Ofsted (2011), *Ages of Concern: Learning Lessons from Serious Case Reviews*; or National Patient Safety Agency (2008), *Independent Investigation of Serious Patient Safety Incidents in Mental Health Services: Good Practice Guidance*; or Brandon et al. (2008b), *Analysing Child Deaths and Serious Injuries through Abuse and Neglect: What Can We Learn?*

**List each key lesson in turn.**

| Use the following table to think through the implications for your practice, as shown in the example below. | What are the practice implications in your context? | What can you do to help ensure that the practice responds positively to that lesson? |
|---|---|---|
| Practitioners overwhelmed by the demands of the job. | More frequent supervision of frontline staff that makes space to discuss their feelings and experiences, not just identify targets. | A manager might be able to directly influence this. A practitioner might decide to ask their manager for a change in their supervision, or for access to different sources of support from a more experienced colleague, for example. |

When it comes to the *implementation* of recommendations, as Downham and Lingham note, it is important to ensure that 'individual local recommendations are not forgotten' (2009: 60) in cases where national implications or common themes generate extensive media attention. The need to assess progress in implementing change following reports is now being increasingly recognized and one example of this would be the review of the extent to which the recommendations arising from the 'J' children case in Edlington have been achieved (Carlile 2012). The range and complexity of recommendations consistently emerging from reviews and inquiries means that these cannot be successfully implemented by a few key staff, but rather require a whole-organization response.

## Effective Risk Systems

Since decision errors can be located in systems, processes and procedures as well as within individual subjective decision making, the 'risk system' has increasingly become a focus of attention. It can be useful to look at this in relation to the following areas:

- the fitness of risk policies and procedures to deliver what they are required to deliver;
- monitoring, audit and quality assurance;
- system oversight.

Risk systems are only as good as the staff who operate them and the managers who ensure they are working properly. Calder (2011) reminds us of the critical role of 'risk controllers', those who are at a sufficient level in the organization to carry out quality assurance of risk systems and who can direct improvements and corrective actions. Although some of the material in this section may be more directly relevant to managers and risk controllers, it is important for all staff to have an understanding of these issues in order to be able to support the development of effective local risk systems.

The organizational characteristics listed below are suggested as indicators of a service that is 'working well':

- serious failures of standards of care are uncommon;
- serious failures of a similar kind do not recur on a future occasion;
- incidents where services have failed in one part of the country are not repeated elsewhere;

- systems are in place which reduce to a minimum the likelihood of serious failure in standards of care;
- attention is also paid to monitoring and reducing levels of less serious incidents. (DoH 2000: 4)

The aim throughout this chapter is to encourage critical thinking about how to develop and sustain effective risk systems that will contribute to achieving these standards of practice.

## *The Fitness of Risk Policies and Procedures to Deliver What is Required of Them*

Earlier chapters have emphasized the importance of professional knowledge, discretion and expertise. These absolutely critical skills need to be used and applied within agreed boundaries, that is, within the agreed policies and procedures of an organization.

Risk policies can do a number of key things. They can state the overall aims and objectives of the agency in responding to a given risk; they provide a framework within which practitioners make their decisions; they allocate roles and responsibilities; and they should allocate resources to risk. In addition, they may state desired outcomes and priorities for risk taking, particularly in respect of expected risk dilemmas, and how differing perspectives on risk are to be reconciled. Well-formulated risk policies may also state minimum competencies for staff, training requirements, review procedures and requirements for staff oversight and supervision (see Titterton 2005: 69–71; Carson and Bain 2008).

Carson and Bain argue that risk policies should be understood as a set of professional standards (important in cases of negligence or risk-management failure) and need to make clear the underpinning values and principles of the agency. Stating this 'service philosophy or value system' is critical to subsequent judgements of the correctness or otherwise of risk decisions by staff (Carson and Bain 2008: 213). If child protection is the core value, then all subsequent decisions by staff will ultimately be judged as to whether they contributed to achieving this core value and key objective. Decisions that do not will be judged very harshly indeed. As noted in the discussion of ethics in chapter 5, tension between competing values and priorities is inherent in social work practice where practitioners have to balance competing rights and risks. While there are no easy solutions, viewing risk policies as professional standards can sometimes help to clarify the most appropriate course of action.

---

**Activity 6.5    Knowledge of Your Local Risk Policy**

It is important to have good knowledge of your organization's risk policy and this activity (for both practitioners and managers) helps you to reflect on that.

- Are you confident that you understand the risk priorities of your organization?
- Do you know what your decisions will be measured against?
- Which aspects of the policy (if any) do you need further information/ guidance about?

If you are applying for jobs or thinking about moving to a new post:

- How much do you know about the risk policies and procedures of the organizations you are hoping to work for?
- Would the quality of an organization's risk policies affect your decision about whether or not to work there?

---

Risk policies are the starting point for 'risk practice' and as such they must be fit for purpose. As Calder (2008a) highlights, however, policies can fail both workers and clients, for example by being under-resourced, overly complicated, procedurally dense with little regard for desirable outcomes, providing conflicting guidance and instruction to staff and being difficult to implement with integrity (e.g. there is no time to do what is required by the policy and short-cuts are constantly taken). In these circumstances, individual blame can be attributed for risk failures that were mainly systemic in nature. It is therefore important for managers, and particularly risk system controllers (i.e. those at a level of policy formation), to review the fitness for purpose of risk policies.

---

**Activity 6.6    Testing Fitness for Purpose**

The previous activity asked you to reflect on your own knowledge of your organization's risk policy. This exercise moves on to help you think about the quality and clarity of that policy.

- Does your risk policy(ies) have a clear statement of aims and objectives?
- Is the underpinning value of the risk policy clear?
- Does it clearly allocate roles and responsibilities?
- Does it indicate how risk dilemmas are to be resolved?
- Does it state minimum staff competence, training requirements and supervision oversight?
- Does it clearly allocate resources?
- Has the policy been clearly explained to staff? (If staff were interviewed about it, would they be able to explain the policy and what they are required to do?)
- Does the policy unhelpfully 'encourage' shortcuts and non-compliance from staff?

If you have answered 'no' to any of the above or you have concerns, consider the following questions:

- Practitioners: how are you going to draw these issues to the attention of managers?
- Managers: what corrective action do you need to take and how can you do this?

Without such corrective actions, the risk policy remains inadequate and potentially a source of risk failure.

## Monitoring, Audit and Quality Assurance

Although monitoring and quality assurance may not initially seem to be a priority topic for social work, it is an important part of the process of evaluating and improving risk practice. For example, collecting 'hard' data (statistics, for example) can complement the 'softer' information that practitioners use in their day-to-day decision making. A useful approach therefore is to think about data as a tool to trigger further enquiry and exploration of practice. A helpful question to consider at this stage would be: 'Does your organization understand that data help you to ask intelligent and pertinent questions rather than just provide a complete picture?' (Fish 2009: 12).

### Knowing what you need to know

It might seem obvious, but taking time to establish clearly what you, your team or organization needs to know is the necessary foundation for any subsequent audit or quality assurance activity. As a starting point, the areas listed below can provide a framework for identifying the questions to ask:

- Processes
  For example: is there any variation in timeliness and completeness of risk assessments at different times of the year? Is there any significant difference in levels of completeness between different types of cases or between different practitioners?
- Outputs
  For example: what proportion of group X is classified as high risk and how does this compare to group Y? What types of intervention or service appear most frequently on care plans for service users assessed as high/low/medium risk?
- Outcomes
  For example: is there a trend of low-risk cases suddenly being escalated up to high risk when a crisis occurs? Are there frequent 'near misses' (see below)?

---

**Activity 6.7   Identifying What you Need to Know**

As explained above, effective auditing and monitoring of practice need to be based on a clear understanding of what information you need to know and why this information is important.

   Consider the risk-assessment and risk-management practice in your team in terms of the areas listed: processes; outputs; outcomes.

- What information is currently being collected?
- How is it shared across your team or organization?
- What use is made of that information and how are those decisions communicated?
- What other information would it be helpful for you to know and what benefit would it bring?

---

*Obtaining what you need to know*

There are a number of techniques for carrying out quality assurance, for example:

- process and procedure compliance audits;
- testing 'information chains' for 'weak links', especially in multi-agency work;

- recording issues and computer data management-sampling over time;
- knowledge and practice audits: do staff know and do the right things? (e.g. inspections);
- staff supervision that is proactive and investigative.

Each of these covers a number of different elements. For example, testing 'information chains' includes not only the availability of specific information sources but also issues such as whether inter-agency communication is based on a shared understanding of risk concepts (Hall and Slembrouck 2009) and whether information transmitted electronically is accurate and up to date (Langan 2009; O'Rourke 2010). Some other suggested approaches are outlined below.

*Looking at good practice*   Carson and Bain argue that looking at good practice is an essential aspect of review and evaluation. 'How do we continue to learn new skills and improve old ones? Do we learn best by having our errors, failings and inadequacies pointed out to us? To an extent, but surely the best, and most, learning comes from being shown what works, how and why it is correct, and what is good practice' (2008: 61). Achieving this requires 'an organizational interest not only in whether good quality products and outcomes have been produced but also in finding out *how* these have been achieved' (Fish 2009: 8). It means having systems and feedback mechanisms in place to identify when good practice occurs, what supports it and what might make it more difficult to attain in particular cases or situations.

*Critical incident reporting and monitoring 'near misses'*   In their discussion of child protection work, Mills and Vine state that one of the key elements of the critical incident approach is the idea that 'errors committed by individuals and agencies should be reported irrespective of the outcome' (1990: 218). While 'error is a normal part of professional practice' (1990: 216), not all mistakes lead to catastrophic outcomes. However, it is important to learn from those errors, whatever the outcome.

The reporting of 'near misses' has become a feature of practice in spheres ranging from aviation to health care (Barach and Small 2000; Department of Health 2000). A 'near miss' can be defined as 'an incident where something could have gone wrong but has been prevented or did go wrong but no serious harm was caused' (Bostock et al. 2005: vi). Information provided by social workers regarding child protection incidents indicated that 'near misses' could occur at any stage of a case (Bostock et al. 2005) and this could equally well apply to those working in mental health, elder care or other social work spheres. Learning can occur either from single incidents or from clusters of 'near misses' (Calder 2008a: 145) which can be a warning sign that problems need to be addressed. There needs to be a balance between taking account of 'near misses' and not being so overly preoccupied with fear of mistakes that people become reluctant to take action.

Questions to consider could include:

- Was this 'near miss' an exceptional event that could not have been predicted or were there signs/triggers that were not identified quickly enough?
- If there has been a cluster of 'near misses', what are the common themes?

---

### Activity 6.8    Case Studies

Consider the following examples of 'near misses' taken from Bostock et al. (2005). For each case, consider:

- What were the key failures that led to the 'near miss'?
- How could/should these have been prevented?
- How do these compare to 'near misses' that you are aware of within your organization?

1    A seven-year-old girl was referred to social services by the fire service. She had been taken to them by her parents to 'teach her a lesson' about fire-setting behaviour (often associated with sexual abuse). The referral was not prioritized and remained unallocated. Two months later, a second referral came from the girl's school, concerning a 10-day-old burn on her hand. The child had explained her injury variously as a carpet burn and as a scratch from her mother. A home visit found the family living in squalor. This led to a child protection conference, both because the burn itself was significant and because of the chronic neglect. Subsequently, following intuitive suspicions about the father, a very experienced worker picked up the case. Determined, she managed to locate 'missing' old files. These revealed significant earlier allegations of sexual abuse, which provided a key to understanding the dynamics of the situation.

> 2　Social services had been working with a family for many years, includ-
> ing looking after the children while the mother was in rehab recover-
> ing from drug addiction. After rehab, though, the mother replaced
> drugs with alcohol. There were drunken parties in her house. Neigh-
> bours, unhappy about the mother's behaviour, had attacked the house.
> Her request to be rehoused was refused. The concern was that the
> children were at risk from neglect. The social workers, who knew the
> mother, were keen to keep the family together because she was caring
> and attentive and had been taking the children out on trips, and the
> children clearly loved their mother. They felt that they had seen a
> positive change in her parenting behaviour and an initial decision was
> made to leave two children in her care. The team leader reminded the
> workers of the 'rule of optimism' and advised caution in taking too
> rosy a view, given the history. Subsequently, on finding the children
> home alone while the mother was out drinking, they were removed
> and taken into foster care.
>
> **Commentary**
> As Bostock et al. note, the first case study relates to problems with referral
> and assessment. It illustrates that 'misinterpretation or misdiagnosis of
> risk is a key feature of safeguarding incidents in general and near misses
> in particular' (2005: 22). The second case shows some of the difficulties
> of working with long-term cases where there may be a 'tendency to give
> people you know "more leeway" than you would those with whom you
> have had no previous involvement' (2005: 32).

Regular reporting of serious incidents and 'near misses' needs to
occur in a working environment in which 'mistakes may be perceived
as *opportunities for learning*' (Beddoe 2010: 11, emphasis added).
This will mean that it is not a 'blaming' activity but a *constructive*
way to improve practice.

*Asking the unasked questions*　Cooperrider, Whitney and Stavros
suggest that '[T]he questions we ask, the things that we choose to
focus on, and the topics we choose to ask questions about determine
what we find' (2008: 103). If this is so, then it will also be the case
that the areas we *don't* ask questions about will remain hidden and
not understood. It is important therefore to consider which aspects
of practice are rarely questioned or challenged. Examples of this
could include: assessments which contain assumptions or judgements

about behaviour of members of particular ethnic groups which is not questioned for fear of seeming racist; or decisions made by the most experienced practitioners in a team who are seen as 'above criticism'.

---

### Activity 6.9   Asking the Unasked Questions

Everyone within a team – students, new practitioners, experienced staff and managers – can contribute to developing practice by asking constructively critical questions. Use the following points as prompts to help you identify some unasked (or infrequently asked) questions:

- Which aspects of practice or performance tend to get 'swept under the carpet'?
- What questions about practice or performance do you think service users and/or their families might most want to ask?
- What questions do you think partner organizations would most like to ask about your agency's practice or performance?
- If you only had one question to ask a senior manager, what would it be?

Now try to complete the table below, identifying (i) a specific question to be asked; and (ii) the way that you would ask the question. This latter will depend on whether it is a question about the practice of specific colleagues, for example, or the performance of a team as a whole. The first three rows relate to the categories of processes, outputs and outcomes discussed above, and you should expand the table for any other topics you might want to add.

|  | Unasked question you think should be asked | How would you ask that question and who would you ask? |
|---|---|---|
| Processes |  |  |
| Outputs |  |  |
| Outcomes |  |  |
| Other |  |  |

Asking such questions can present dilemmas; for example, it may reveal practice that you or others think is inappropriate. Some of the ethical issues surrounding such challenges were discussed in chapter 5 (e.g. Activity 5.7) and, while it may be difficult to avoid the tensions they create, the aim should be to keep the focus on improving rather than blaming. The questions should be asked in a way that contributes to learning within the organization. Avoiding the difficult questions is rarely a successful approach in the long term and it is better to try to address problems early rather than wait for them to be highlighted in a case review following a major incident.

## System Oversight

Risk controllers require adequate reports from team leaders, frontline operational staff, those who make risk decisions and those who provide immediate support, advice and guidance to these staff. Risk controllers need to ensure that the reporting up structures are sound, and that they have sufficient oversight of key areas of practice. Risk practice also requires critical organizational structures to ensure that it can be delivered well and there are resources sufficient to the task.

Creating sufficient oversight of the risk system requires:

- oversight of decision makers and decision supporters;
- review of working relationships, principles, protocols, procedures;
- proactive review, fitness for purpose of organizational structures;
- sufficiency and quality of resources for risk;
- fitness of staff to make risk decisions. (See e.g. Carson and Bain 2008; Calder 2011; Kemshall and Wilkinson 2011)

However, sufficient oversight does not come easily. We can all be distracted by immediate day-to-day concerns in the workplace, or spend time on tasks and activities that we find comfortable, easy and rewarding. Creating a structured and focused approach to risk, rather than a merely responsive one, takes effort but is likely to ensure a greater organizational fitness for risk. The following exercise encourages a critical review of how assurance reporting is currently operating in your agency. Negative answers signal lack of fitness and require corrective action. The second point invites you to consider whether a re-balancing of your oversight activities is required. Oversight should follow risk concerns, and it is interesting to consider whether this is actually the case or whether your time is being spent on less important tasks.

---

**Activity 6.10 Improving System Oversight**

This exercise is primarily for risk controllers and managers and is intended to help you think about the strengths/areas for improvement in your oversight of risk systems.
Consider the following questions and identify any gaps.

- How do I gain assurance that processes and procedures are right and are being followed as I would wish?
- How can I create sufficient oversight of all my areas of responsibility? What do I do the most and is this appropriate? What re-balancing do I need to do?
- Are the 'reporting up' structures to me of sufficient quality for me to know what I need to know?

Consider the corrective actions you can take.

---

Risk controllers should aim to develop systems and cultures in which it is 'harder for people to do something wrong and easier for them to do it right' (Institute of Medicine 1999: 2, cited in Munro 2010a: 1141). The following tips for good practice are suggested:

- Know how those below you are assured!
- Ask structured and focused questions about your area of operation.
- Test a process or procedure – sample, observe, obtain feedback.
- Respond to variations, inconsistency and 'poor' performance signals.
- 'Scrutiny time' should follow risk(s) – try to 'apportion' accordingly.
- Show active interest rather than just responding to demands.
- Seek a 360-degree view. How do others see your department? How do partners view your service delivery?
- Finally, remember – risk systems are only as good as you make them!

## Learning and Improving

The previous discussions have highlighted the need for effective systems which both set out the frameworks for practice while also enabling change to take place where needed for improvement. This can be triggered by learning from positive practice, negative events or routine monitoring and audit. For all this information to have an impact on practice, organizations need good feedback loops (Munro 2010a) and this is particularly important where individuals within organizations do not necessarily directly experience the consequences of some of their decisions (Senge 2006: 23). This may occur where assessment teams are separate from intervention teams, for example. If it is difficult for practitioners to see the results of their actions, then organizations need to have systems for monitoring outcomes and giving feedback to decision makers.

All the activities and processes described above are likely to reveal gaps in knowledge and skills for both individuals and organizations which need to be addressed if practice is to develop (Bissell 2012). In thinking about how to promote improvement, Whyte provides a helpful reminder that 'practitioners require what has been described as "deep" as opposed to "surface" learning' (Whyte 2009: 203). This involves many of the elements outlined in earlier chapters – understanding theory, knowing the local context for practice, reflecting on successes, problems and 'near misses' and then applying all of this appropriately to individual cases. Achieving this kind of depth in practice requires a combination of professional knowledge and experience plus an organizational commitment to promoting and applying learning, as illustrated in Figure 6.2.

**Figure 6.2** Framework of knowledge and organizational commitment
*Source*: adapted from Kemshall et al., 'Assessment and Management of Risk', training resource for the Risk Management Authority, 2007 (used with the permission of the Risk Management Authority).

What might this look like in practice? Calder (2011: 209) suggests that learning organizations should ideally have a working culture which:

- promotes openness, creativity and experimentation among members;
- encourages members to acquire, share and process information;
- provides the freedom to try new things, risk failure and learn from mistakes;
- celebrates and shares good practice;
- systematically gathers views from service users and carers and uses them to influence service planning;
- creates opportunities for members to reflect and learn from new evidence and research.

This emphasis on learning is essential because, as Munro rightly argues, '[r]educing prescription without creating a learning system will not secure the desired improvements in the system' (2011: 10).

## Summary and Conclusion

High-profile risk failures in social work, social care and offender management inevitably raise serious questions about the quality of practice. As has been said many times, however, risk is intrinsic to social work and cannot be eliminated. Even with the best systems, some things will go wrong, events will be unpredictable, decisions which seemed good at the time may turn out to be problematic. But there are of course also many examples of good risk work happening on a day-to-day basis that are rarely reported.

Review and evaluation of risk work is essential to both encourage good practice and challenge poor risk-decision making. This chapter has highlighted the following key factors:

- Improving practice is a shared responsibility between individuals and organizations.

- A systems perspective provides a useful focus on the complex range of personal, social and organizational factors which influence risk-decision making.
- Risk systems require regular review/update.
- Risk controllers have a critical role in overseeing risk systems and implementing changes.
- Organizations need to be alert to different sources for learning about risk practice – inquiries, inspections, routine data monitoring, audit, critical reflection.
- Opportunities for improvement are increased when organizations create a working culture that focuses on learning rather than blaming.

Risk systems are only as good as you make them.

The aim should be to move towards creating an 'open, confident, self-regulating system where professionals are continually asking how they can improve rather than a system clouded by fear' (Gove 2012: 2). Achieving this will help protect the interests and welfare of both service users and wider society.

### Further Reading

Fish, S., Munro, E. and Bairstow, S. (2008) *Learning Together to Safeguard Children: Developing a Multi-Agency Systems Approach for Case Reviews.* London: Social Care Institute for Excellence. This provides a useful guide to making the most of the SCR process.

Sidebotham, P. et al. (2010) *Learning from Serious Case Reviews: Report of a Research Study on the Methods of Learning Lessons Nationally from Serious Case Reviews.* London: Department for Education. Gives a useful perspective on implementing lessons learned from inquiries or reviews.

Stanley, N. and Manthorpe, J. (eds) (2004) *The Age of the Inquiry: Learning and Blaming in Health and Social Care.* London: Routledge. Provides an in-depth review covering both specific inquiries (in child protection, mental health, abuse of people with learning disabilities and abuse/neglect of older people) and discussion of broader debates regarding the nature and purpose of the inquiry process.

### Useful Websites

National Confidential Inquiry into Suicide and Homicide by People with Mental Illness: www.medicine.manchester.ac.uk/mentalhealth/research/ suicide/prevention/nci/, accessed 28 February 2013.

Serious Case Reviews, NSPCC Factsheet: www.nspcc.org.uk/Inform/research/questions/serious_case_reviews_wda70252.html, accessed 28 February 2013.

The Studies in the Safeguarding Research Initiative, Department for Education: www.education.gov.uk/researchandstatistics/research/scri/b0076846/the-studies-in-the-safeguarding-research-initiative, accessed 28 February 2013.

The Victoria Climbié Inquiry report, Lord Laming: www.dh.gov.uk/en/Publicationsandstatistics/Publications/PublicationsPolicyAndGuidance/DH_4008654, accessed 28 February 2013.

# 7

# Managing Self in the Organizational Context

The organizations within which individuals are seeking to make the best possible decisions about risk can be understood as complex adaptive systems (Munro 2010c). For such complex systems to work well, it is important that feedback and learning is encouraged throughout. As chapter 6 explores in some depth, practitioners should be enabled to use their professional judgement and to share their experiences honestly, so that these can be used as an opportunity for learning, individually and collectively. This may not be the consistent experience of individuals working within organizations, faced with routinized responses to risk (see chapter 3), struggling with limited resources and feeling that blame is a more likely response if they share difficulties in practice.

One of the reasons why managing self is so important is that risk-decision making in conditions of uncertainty can be stressful, negatively impacting on the quality of that decision making. Anxiety about making the best decision and about managing potential outcomes may interact with anxiety linked to high workloads and limited resources. Experiences of unhelpful levels of stress may lead to reduced performance, burn-out and decisions to leave this area of work (Coffey, Dugdill and Tattersall 2004). This chapter will focus on what individuals can do, and what support they should seek, to enable them to work at their best, within the reality of their working context. Equal attention should also be paid to how organizations should be structured to minimize unhelpful stress and to make the most of staff skills and abilities (Beddoe 2010). As chapter 6 has discussed, organizations should be open to learning, so that those aspects which are working well can be embedded in practice and practitioners and service users can play their part in influencing organizational development.

## Self-Management Skills

An individual's ability to manage themselves successfully in social work settings which are charged with assessing and managing risk will depend on a number of individual factors, including those in the following activity.

| Activity 7.1   Your Own Characteristics | | |
|---|---|---|
| Use the following table to note your first conclusions about what personal characteristics and skills help you manage successfully. | | |
| **Individual factors supporting effective self-management** | **How does this factor help me manage myself well at work?** | **How might I strengthen this factor so that my self-management can improve?** |
| Motivation to engage with the social work task of risk assessment and management | | |
| Knowledge, skill and ability to engage in reflective practice | | |
| Resilience and ability to cope with stress | | |
| Ability to understand and work with your own emotions and those of others | | |

These characteristics and skills can help individuals learn from the challenges they face, develop their practice knowledge and skill for future tasks and be persistent in the face of adversity, while being realistic about the limits of their ability to manage risk. We will now explore each of them in more depth before considering some of the strategies that individuals may find helpful.

## Motivation to Engage with the Task

Why do practitioners want to work with individuals and families where they have to make anxiety-provoking decisions about risk? Stevens et al. (2010) looked at the motivations for becoming a social worker. They found that helping individuals and pursuing interesting work were the most common among a range of career motivations in which altruistic reasons predominated. Collins (2008) cites a number of studies which indicate that statutory social workers are committed to their job and find their contact with service users rewarding, believing that they are able to make a difference. It may be that individuals who hold a strong commitment to working with and helping others are more likely to persevere and to survive in the face of difficult challenges.

Organizations can support this motivation to engage by enabling staff to have a sense of control and by valuing good practice. 'Sustained commitment is also more likely if the individual sees their own personal values and beliefs aligned with those of the organization. Alignment is rarely total and there can, for example, be conflicts over what is in the best interest of service users, or conflicts about how resources should be used' (Hill 2010). Practitioners work out their own practical versions of policy in conditions of high caseloads, limited resources and where organizations have a narrow focus on achieving specific targets (Evans and Harris 2004; Kemshall 2010a). Carey and Foster (2011) looked at what they describe as deviant social work, where individuals depart from policy for varied and individualistic reasons that are difficult for organizations to engage with and manage. If individuals are instead encouraged openly and actively to seek to change unhelpful practice contexts, their motivation may increase because they will retain a stronger belief that they can continue to work in ways that match their values. This is important because individual adaptations of policy can have dangers attached to them.

Chapter 5 discussed in more depth the importance of individuals operating with integrity, helping to ensure that decision making is carried out in good faith and that discretion is exercised within a framework of rights and duties. Such individuals are also likely to feel a greater sense of commitment and security in role. Banks (2009) suggests that there are a number of components of professional integrity:

- standards;
- a set of moral values and beliefs; and
- critical reflection on decision making.

She suggests that the third element is needed so that the opposing traps of reducing practice to narrow minimum standards or on the other hand to over-individualized decisions about what is right are both avoided.

---

**Activity 7.2   Using Critical Reflection**

This book has encouraged you throughout to engage in the third form of integrity: critical reflection. This activity asks you to critically reflect on Banks's components of integrity as they apply to a particular decision. It is best done on a real risk decision you have made or been closely involved in. It would provide a useful discussion starter in supervision.
   To what extent was the decision guided by:

- abiding by standards set for this decision;
- putting into practice a set of moral values and beliefs;
- active critical reflection as the decision was being made?

Was an appropriate balance struck between each of the above? If not, what were the implications for decision making?

---

## Knowledge, Skills and Reflection on Practice

Critical reflection is important, not just for supporting integrity in decision making but for developing practice skills and knowledge. Those practitioners who feel confident in their application of skills and who are clear about their reasons for action are likely to sustain their motivation. Organizations should support reflection and be good at recognizing and rewarding the development of professional skill and expertise (Russ, Lonne and Darlington 2009).
   Chapter 2 made plain the importance of practice based on the best possible current knowledge about a range of risk factors and their implications for individuals, in context. Risk-decision makers should be confident that they know enough about:

- research findings and theory in their area of practice;
- policy and process;
- practice realities in a given agency or locality;
- local communities, drawing on an understanding of diversity and difference.

Knowledge should be matched by characteristics and skills, such as emotional self-management and persistence, that help to use that knowledge constructively in practice (Munro 2010a).

Risk-decision making requires practitioners to bring together policy knowledge, formal knowledge and practice knowledge that comes from engagement with service users. The ability to bring these different understandings together is developed best by a reflective practitioner who is able to look critically at his/her actions and their effects and to use that reflection to inform actions and decisions in the future. Donnellan and Jack (2010) suggest that, as well as reflecting *on action*, it is helpful to engage in reflection *in action*, that is, to step back from actions being taken to think critically about the process, so that practice can be amended in the moment.

Reflection can focus on the practical application of theory to practice. It can make good decision making more likely if biased judgements are uncovered and challenged and if the individual is willing to learn from what they do well and from their mistakes. Reflection needs therefore to be appropriately self-critical, thinking through accepted knowledge, how the practitioner has applied that knowledge, what skills were used and how all of this was experienced by service users. A wider critical perspective is also relevant, challenging accepted assumptions and looking at what is done from a variety of perspectives, including critical attention to the social and political context of decision making (Evans and Hardy 2010).

Besides developing individual skills, this wider perspective and the learning that grows from using critical reflection in and on action can play a constructive role in the development of policy and practice. It should be part of the deep learning discussed in chapter 6, allowing practitioners to sustain a sense that what they are doing is worthwhile and makes a difference. Just having the right skill and knowledge is not enough. An individual also needs to believe that they are able to put those skills into practice and that doing so will produce desired outcomes. Reflection and the developments that flow from it should also support the growth of positive self-efficacy. There is a considerable body of evidence that self-efficacy beliefs have a significant effect on what is achieved in many life areas, including success at sport and achievements at work.

> People's beliefs in their efficacy have diverse effects. Such beliefs influence the courses of action people choose to pursue, how much effort they put forth in given endeavours, how long they will persevere in the face of obstacles and failures, their resilience to adversity, whether their thought patterns are self-hindering or self-aiding, how much stress and depression they experience in coping with taxing environmental demands, and the level of accomplishments they realize. (Bandura 1997: 3)

This quote suggests that an optimistic sense of personal efficacy is crucial, influencing a wide range of behaviours.

---

**Activity 7.3   Your Personal Efficacy Beliefs and Their Effects**

This table cites some of the effects of efficacy beliefs found by Bandura and gives examples of the differences they might make to behaviour in social work.

|  | Effects of a positive perception of personal efficacy – some examples | Effects of a negative perception of personal efficacy – some examples |
| --- | --- | --- |
| Choices | Will be more willing to take on challenging and difficult cases. | Chooses to procrastinate and avoid difficult decisions. |
| Effort | Puts effort into the quality of their assessment and management practice. Seeks and acts on feedback about quality. | Limits practice to the narrower demands of agency process. |
| Perseverance | Seeks out missing information, keeps trying to involve challenging service users. | Gives up when faced with obstacles. |

| Resilience | Is motivated by appropriate levels of stress and able to put strategies into place to manage unhelpful stressors. | Is incapacitated by stress and anxiety, fails to make decisions, or makes them without real thought. |
|---|---|---|
| Thought patterns | 'I can make a difference, this effort will be worthwhile.' 'If I try again with a different approach, the outcome may be more positive.' | 'What's the point? What I do doesn't make any difference.' 'I tried but there is nothing to be done.' |

Look at the table and think about your own professional practice. You should be operating in the first column: can you identify times when this is clearly the case for you and times when you have strayed into the second column? Think about these specific questions:

- What supports your positive sense of efficacy? Is it your perception of your skills? Do you also think about the outcomes your actions are able to achieve?
- In contrast, when you operate with a negative sense of efficacy, what part does a lack of faith in your own skills play? What part is influenced by a lack of confidence that you can use existing skills to achieve outcomes?
- When you operate with a positive sense of efficacy, what impact does that have on the quality of work you do and the effort you put into tasks?

## Coping with Stress: The Importance of Resilience

Working with risk in social work will always have the potential to make a negative impact on the thinking and well-being of staff. We have acknowledged the difficulty of decision making in conditions of uncertainty. Role ambiguity, poor or unclear boundaries and accountability can add to this sense of uncertainty and bring with it the fear of blame, all of which can increase stress. The way in which practice is structured can also impact on the perception of stress. For example:

- over-fragmentation of service delivery with initial referral, assessment and risk planning carried out in turn by different parts of the organization can lead to deskilling;
- overly prescriptive practice may distort how workers spend their time, adding to perceptions of overload and a lack of space in which to reflect. (Donnellan and Jack 2010)

Social workers working with individuals and families who are experiencing pain and distress sometimes face challenging and aggressive behaviours from service users. It would be unrealistic to expect workers themselves to be exempt from feelings of stress and anxiety (Howe 2008). It is important, however, that stress does not lead to negativity or engender a sense of hopelessness. Workers should develop strategies to operate professionally, focusing on strengths to counter adverse experiences. Resilient workers will be better able to overcome adversity and ideally will learn from and grow professionally as a result of difficult experiences.

Efficacy rooted in self-confidence, underpinned by a professional knowledge base and the ability to apply that knowledge appropriately, will support the individual's resilience to challenges and failures. Individuals also need self-management skills to function at their best in difficult contexts. Mechanisms for coping with excessive levels of stress and for building resilience can be divided into two broad types (Collins 2008). Both are relevant to stress management in the context of risk-decision making.

- Problem-solving coping will seek to reduce the source of stress. This may include taking professional steps to plan and prioritize, gathering more information, clarifying the basis of your decision making by discussing it with others and taking sometimes difficult decisions to resolve stressful situations. This problem-solving may be carried out by the individual but will often take place in the context of formal supervision or peer support.
- Emotion-focused coping will improve the ability of the individual to manage their own difficult feelings. This may include developing cognitive skills to reduce the likelihood of unhelpful dwelling on negative thoughts and worst outcomes. More balanced and positive thinking about a stressful situation may help an individual re-engage with a focused problem-solving set of strategies. Again, emotion-focused coping is often facilitated by supportive individuals or organizational processes like supervision.

---

**Activity 7.4   Managing Stress**

Think of a specific time when you were feeling under significant stress. This could be in relation to any aspect of your life or related specifically to work (including, of course, your current situation).

• What were the most significant sources of stress?
• List the major strategies you used to cope with that stress.
• To what extent were your strategies focused on managing your own emotional reaction?
• To what extent were your strategies directed at reducing the sources of stress?
• Was the balance right given that particular situation? If not, what could you have done differently?
• How were these strategies supported by your organization? Could they have helped in different ways?

---

Organizations should avoid the trap of paying attention only to those who are struggling to cope. Russ, Lonne and Darlington (2009) suggest that it may be more helpful to focus on why it is that the majority of staff members continue to function, even when the situation is very challenging. They argue that a focus on strengths and resilience will be more productive for both individuals and organizations. Similarly, concerns that we are working within a blame – rather than a learning – culture will diminish if organizations focus on learning from mistakes and building strengths and efficacy in their workforce. Fostering resilience should produce staff better able to cope with future challenges.

Russ, Lonne and Darlington suggest that 'increased use of reflective practice, supervision, ongoing learning, and collaborative peer support may be useful in promoting resilience in child protection staff, by strengthening workers' sense of control, fostering their commitment through valuing client-related work, and helping them to manage challenges successfully' (2009: 331). Reflective practice therefore, while not a panacea, supports resilience as well as the quality of decision making.

### Understanding and working with emotions

Earlier chapters have covered the importance of awareness in practitioners of their own thinking and the thinking of service users in order to make good decisions about risk. Thinking is also influenced by an individual's feelings and by the ability to understand one's own and others' emotional reactions. This ability is sometimes termed 'emotional intelligence' (Goleman 1996). There is an ongoing debate about the extent to which this ability is a measurable trait as implied by the word 'intelligence'. In order to reflect the importance of continuing to develop relevant skills, the terms 'emotional competence' or 'emotional literacy' may be more helpful. Emotional literacy includes knowledge of emotions, the ability to recognize and respond empathically to emotions in others and an awareness of the causes, triggers and expressions of emotions in ourselves and others (C. Knight 2012, personal communication). Emotional competence includes 'the ability to monitor one's own and others' feelings and emotions, to discriminate among them, and to use this information to guide one's thinking and action' (Morrison 2007: 250).

These abilities are important for risk assessors and managers in social work. Understanding and responding to feelings is also influenced by context. In social work, a working environment that does not show responsiveness to individual practitioners' emotions may be less likely to foster that kind of responsiveness to service users. Workers who, as individuals, lack empathy and self-awareness can also present some of the most difficult performance management dilemmas for organizations. If they feel threatened by constructive challenge, or are made anxious by change, without understanding their own responses, they will find it harder to deal professionally with difficulties. This can negatively affect those around them.

As well as supporting work with service users, emotional literacy also supports effective working relationships with colleagues and with professionals from other agencies. Understanding your own emotional responses can positively affect self-management in conditions of adversity. For example, anxiety can influence where individuals focus their attention and make it harder for practitioners to connect and work collaboratively. Workers need to strike a skilful balance in their relationships with others, including service users. Howe (2008) suggests that they need to balance:

- *intra*personal skills, self-awareness and self-management;
- *inter*personal skills, awareness of others and relationship skills.

These skills must be used with a clear sense of the purpose and desired outcomes of the relationship to avoid the traps of, on the one hand, a failure to engage and, on the other, over-identification and collusion.

---

**Activity 7.5   Using Self-Management Skills 1**

Read this example and then complete the reflection:
A student social worker and a more experienced colleague are at a home visit to an adult service user. This service user has a past history of aggressive behaviour and is experiencing problems with his current living arrangements. During their discussions, the service user jumps to his feet and starts pacing around the room, shouting and gesticulating. The student experiences feelings of fear and anxiety and a desire to end the interaction immediately or to hand over to her colleague. However, she is able to reflect in action and understand that, while her concern for her safety is valid, some of her fear is due to her own performance anxiety – can she handle this interaction skilfully? She is also aware that, while the behaviour of the service user is aggressive, the individual concerned is also responding to quite acute feelings of anxiety.

As a result the worker chooses not to end the interview, or to hand over to her colleague, but to tell the service user that she can see that he is very worried and that she understands how upsetting this situation is for him. She is also able to appear confident and to tell the service user that she needs him to speak more quietly and slowly if she is to be able to understand his worries properly. She is able to persevere until the service user is once again seated and the discussion can proceed more constructively.

The example above simply demonstrates the use of some fundamental social work skills. List the self-management skills that you perceive the student was able to use during this reflection in action, both intra- and interpersonal.

---

You may have recognized that this student drew on intrapersonal skills by being self-aware about the range of sources for her own emotional response and therefore finding that response more manageable. She was able to keep her behaviour focused on the service user, not just on her own concerns.

She drew on interpersonal skills by validating the feelings of the other, continuing to demonstrate respect and concern and listening to the other person. She was also able to appropriately express the effects of the service user's behaviour on her and to challenge that constructively, regaining some control.

**Activity 7.6 Using Self-Management Skills 2**

Now think about a difficult interaction of your own, reflecting on the actions you took at the time:

• What inter- and intrapersonal skills did you draw on?
• What skills, if any, could you have made more use of at the time?

## Self-Management Skills and Risk

It is important to acknowledge the particular challenges inherent in working with risk. Emotional responses to the work can lead to avoidance of difficult decisions, or workers who become so intent on their own self-preservation that this is the major influence on the choices they make (Calder 2008b). Unhelpful thinking patterns, for example, ruminating (constantly thinking about difficulties), can emerge as a result of the work (Clarke 2006). A practitioner facing a decision about whether to remove a child from a family may ruminate on the case at work and outside. This may lead to increased anxiety and even depression, which in turn may affect engagement in problem-solving and outcome-focused behaviours (Nolen-Hoeksema, Wisco and Lyubomosicsky 2008). Brandon et al. (2008b) found that in situations of hostility workers often froze and failed to complete assessments. A worker who feels anxious and depressed may seek to attribute blame for those feelings. They may blame the organization and, as a result, start to take unhelpful shortcuts, ignore standards and requirements or just 'go through the motions'. They may blame the service users, resulting in negative thinking and perceptions that unjustly affect the judgements they make about individuals. There should be a balance between reason and emotional understanding: critical reflection can help to effectively manage that balance (Munro 2011).

The analogy of an iceberg can be really helpful in supporting critical reflection on risk-decision making. It draws our attention to influences on decisions that are powerful but that lie under the immediately observable surface of behaviour. How people think about the world, how they behave and how they feel are interrelated; the individual in turn affects the world around them which of course also has impacts on them. What is immediately observable is only the 'tip of the iceberg'. The thoughts and feelings that are influencing actions may be less apparent (Wilkinson 2011).

---

**Activity 7.7  What is Happening 'Under the Surface'**

Use the diagram of the iceberg in Figure 7.1 to think about 'under the surface' elements that may influence you. You might reflect on a particular difficult practice example and use the diagram and the questions for analysis. Alternatively, you could analyse one of the case examples cited earlier in this book.

- Identify specific thoughts and feelings that were associated with the risk-decision making in this case.
- How did those thoughts and feelings interact and how might they have influenced actions?
- What effect was this likely to have on, for example, other service users and colleagues?
- Does this suggest any changes in behaviour?
- How would behavioural change be best supported by changes below the surface in thoughts and feelings?
- What steps could be taken to bring those changes about?

As well as applying this thinking to a specific case, you can use the iceberg analogy to help you identify common patterns of thinking, behaviour and emotions that you slip into when making difficult decisions.

---

As Morrison (2007: 259) points out, 'maturity in help seeking skills and attitudes' is important for social work. The remainder of this chapter explores the steps that individuals can take to manage their own 'iceberg'.

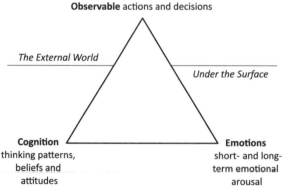

**Figure 7.1**  The iceberg model

## Taking Steps to Support Organizational Survival

There is unlikely to be one single strategy that ensures that a practitioner is able to thrive as an effective risk-decision maker. Instead, the factors discussed in the first part of the chapter suggest a number of strategies that might make a difference.

### *Working with peers*

The safeguarding peer review programme involves representatives from other authorities undertaking a review of practice in a given area. Programme evaluation suggests that peer review can produce real benefits, for example in commitment, learning and reflective practice and staff morale. As one local authority interviewee pointed out, 'It's very easy to get very caught up in your own organization and the way you are doing things. To have somebody else from outside come in . . . stops you from getting too narrowly focused . . . helps you look beyond the organization and say, actually, we could do this differently' (Martin and Jeffes 2011: 4).

Findings suggest that involvement in formal peer review can help organizations and the individuals involved in the process think differently. Peer support and review can also operate at less formal levels, for example, colleagues giving feedback on reports before they are sent to external bodies. Done well, a focused review from trusted colleagues can help to draw out examples of good practice or ways in which it could be improved. The importance of routes that help individuals learn from good practice, as well as from things that go wrong, is explored in more depth in chapter 6.

Relationships with peers are important for other reasons. There will be times when individuals need support from colleagues because of a particularly difficult case, or because other pressures (sometimes outside work) impact on their ability to function well. Formal peer support programmes and co-working on challenging cases are important for resilience (Russ, Lonne and Darlington 2009). Colleagues can make a difference to how effectively someone may 'weather the storm'; however, it is important that colleagues work within a supportive culture (Clarke 2008). There is a danger if one staff member becomes the only source of support for someone else. 'The goal is not to become a sole provider in the workplace but to help it become a cultural norm' (Koprowska 2008: 163). 'The clear message . . . is that support from colleagues is a significant buffer against stress and that social work organizations should commit themselves to making time available for support meetings as part of routine work patterns, not as an optional "add-on"' (Collins 2008: 1183). Individuals, in turn, have to make the most of any opportunities, using them in ways that support the quality of practice. Individuals also need to develop and sustain their own opportunities to access support and learning from peers.

---

### Activity 7.8   Informal Discussions

Think through recent informal, but work-related, conversations you have had with colleagues or, if you are a student, with fellow students. If possible, you could focus on a discussion of cases where risk decisions were relevant. What did you get out of those conversations?

- Did they reassure you and confirm your own conclusions?
- Did they provide any knowledge or skills-based advice that was useful?
- Did they help you think differently?
- Which of these or other elements helped you practise more effectively, and how? Did any of them not support improved practice?

---

### Supervision

More formal routes for support are also essential, a key location being the supervisory relationship between line manager and member of staff. For many workers, however, supervision has become more managerial in focus, with an emphasis on meeting targets and ensuring compliance, rather than on encouraging reflective practice (Noble and Irwin 2009). Good risk practice does require clear accountability and an unambiguous sense of what is expected in order to provide a secure space within which practitioners can engage with challenging and sometimes chaotic lives. Accountability is not enough, however, as practitioners also need to be able to take decisions confidently in situations of uncertainty, where correct solutions are debatable.

Eadie and Canton (2002) point up the tension between increasing standardization of practice and the need to exercise judgement in decision making, especially when working with individuals with complex needs. They suggest that the most effective practice will include high accountability and great discretion. This balance between accountability and support for discretion can describe best practice in supervision where accountability, reflection and learning are essential components. This can be delivered through a supervisory relationship, or through more complex processes which allow the reflective supervision of practice to be at least partially led by, for example, a senior practitioner.

Individuals who receive such supervision will have the security of distinct boundaries and expectations, while developing as reflective practitioners. This kind of supervision needs explicit expectations about behaviour within the supervisory relationship. The power relationships within supervision are not equal; supervisors have the responsibility for managing its content and direction. Supervisees, however, also have responsibility and influence and need to be 'active in order to gain the support they need' (Hill 2010: 60).

- Accountability can be supported by practitioners who bring evidence of good practice to supervision and are active in raising concerns about practice or about the context in which it occurs. Supervisors should monitor practice and discuss the results with the individual concerned. They should also seek to change unhelpful policies outside supervision and to help manage resource limitations.
- Learning and development can be supported by supervisors who use skills to encourage learning from best, as well as problematic, practice and who support this by other contacts with the practitioner and their cases, for example through observation of practice and co-working. Practitioners should bring to supervision a willingness to discuss their feelings, thinking and actions. They should avoid a passive approach which expects the supervisor to take the decision for them and should actively press for reflective opportunities.

---

### Activity 7.9  Making the Most of Supervision

Use the quadrant in Figure 7.2 to think about your own experience as a recipient of supervision, or as a person providing it for others.

- Where in the quadrant do most of your sessions sit?
- What changes, if any, would you like to see?
- How will you go about achieving those changes?

---

**Figure 7.2**   Accountability, reflection and learning, and best practice

Supervision should apply learning to specific cases and should help to identify, through reflection, generalized learning from practice experience. It should highlight where there is a need for further knowledge and skill development. Some of that practice development can be achieved through supervision but other opportunities will be necessary.

### Learning opportunities

Positive self-efficacy should not only value existing skills but also ongoing learning. Individuals or teams who have a very strong sense of efficacy risk becoming complacent and may forget that they still need to learn. Learning and challenge are important to avoid over-confidence, as well as to improve the quality of practice. Practitioners need to be aware of developments in thinking and practice and to be honest about gaps in their knowledge and skill so that they can take steps to learn more and to address those gaps. Case discussions focused on quality are one way in which learning needs can be identified; team discussions about practice may also allow learning needs to emerge.

Access to appropriate formal and less formal learning should also be enabled. Case discussions can themselves provide opportunities for learning. Observing or co-working with colleagues (from one's own or another organization) who possess different knowledge and skills is another potential route. The success of these and more traditional training-based learning opportunities will depend in part on their relevance to the practitioner's learning needs and in part on the practitioner's willingness to be open to learning and to reflect on practice. Success will also depend on whether the application of learning to practice is supported by supervisors and others. Learning is about much more than simply taking on information: it should be an active and purposeful process that helps individuals to bring about real changes in their practice. It should not be a dull or dutiful process but one that is exciting and challenging (Baker, Kelly and Wilkinson 2011).

---

**Activity 7.10    Making the Most of Learning Opportunities**

Next time you engage with a learning opportunity ask yourself:

- What aspects of this are relevant to me?
- Am I open to this learning? How can I improve my openness?
- What can I do and what help can I seek to make sure that I put this learning into practice?

---

## Life outside work

The danger that members of staff involved in challenging areas of practice might lock themselves into unhelpful ruminating patterns of thought, with implications for risk-decision making, was identified earlier. Factors and circumstances outside the workplace may affect this. For example, younger, less experienced practitioners may be more vulnerable to unhelpful rumination, and they may also be affected by personal circumstances, such as living alone (Clarke 2006).

It is important therefore that practitioners pay attention to their general well-being, maintaining an appropriate balance between work and their personal lives and finding support and positive experiences outside the workplace. Practitioners who are in good health are likely to be less susceptible to stress, so whatever steps individuals can take to manage their own physical and emotional health will be of benefit, albeit indirectly, to the quality of practice. Clarke (2008) talks about simple steps, such as ensuring regular brief breaks and taking exercise at lunchtime, as possible strategies to promote professional resilience.

| Activity 7.11   Strategies for Self-Management in the Organization | |
|---|---|
| Use the table below to think about each of the four listed strategies for organizational self-management, answering the question in the second column. | |
| Strategies for organizational self-management | In your current situation:<br>• Which of these strategies is functioning well?<br>• How does that help your ability to work effectively with risk?<br>• What changes would you like to happen and what can you do to bring those changes about? |
| • Relationships with peers | |
| • Supervision | |
| • Learning opportunities | |
| • Life outside of work | |

## Conclusion

Reflective practice emerges as a key support for individuals managing in what can be difficult and uncertain practice contexts. It can encourage building strengths and self-efficacy and can help with emotional, as well as cognitive and behavioural, elements of practice. This can assist individuals to cope with difficult challenges by engaging appropriate problem-solving and good self-management skills to control their own anxieties.

Individuals have to learn when they need to seek help and how to actively pursue the help that they need. Organizations should support this, providing a balance between accountability, learning and development and ensuring that helpful policies, practice standards, supervision and learning opportunities are available.

FURTHER READING

Each of the following articles helpfully explores aspects of this thinking in more depth.

Collins, S. (2008) 'Statutory social workers: stress, job satisfaction, coping, social support and individual differences', *British Journal of Social Work* 38: 1173–93.

Morrison, T. (2007) 'Emotional intelligence, emotion and social work: context, characteristics, complications and contribution', *British Journal of Social Work* 37: 245–63.

Munro, E. (2010) 'Learning to reduce risk in child protection', *British Journal of Social Work* 40: 1135–51.

# Conclusion

Risk is a feature in many different types of decisions – from routine aspects of everyday practice to high-profile cases that cause great anxiety. As has been shown throughout this book, the task of assessing and managing risk often necessitates difficult choices, for example between potential benefits and possible harms. The decisions that are made can have life-changing consequences.

It is helpful to think about risk in social work using these broad categories:

- those risks which people pose to others;
- those risks to which people are exposed;
- risks that allow people to make some of their own choices.

To manage these risks, practitioners have to exercise 'good judgement' in order to make decisions which are well informed, balanced, reasoned, critical and which avoid bias and discrimination. Assessors also have to deal with ethical dilemmas thrown up by risk decisions and act with honesty and integrity. This is clearly a difficult task, requiring high levels of professional skill. This book has aimed to assist practitioners with the challenge of making positive, thoughtful, robust and ethical decisions about risk.

## Assessing Potential Risks

Risk decisions will always involve a degree of uncertainty as, by definition, it is never possible to be completely sure what might happen in the future. Focusing on the following key components, however, provides a solid basis for assessing potential risks:

• the likelihood of an event occurring;
• the extent of harm or benefit involved in any potential outcome.

Different social work organizations will have different frameworks, rules and procedures for undertaking risk assessment. These can be useful in defining the scope of the task but practitioners still need to use their professional skills and judgement, for example in knowing how to apply guidance in a specific case. Ideally, risk-assessment practice should combine 'aspects of professionalism (e.g. using knowledge and skills) with issues of procedural compliance' (Baker and Wilkinson 2011: 15).

In making assessments, practitioners therefore require the relevant knowledge for their specific area of practice. This will include those risk factors indicated by research as most closely associated with particular harmful outcomes. Judgements will, however, need to consider not just the existence of a risk factor but how different factors interact with each other and the patterns of causation that make a harmful outcome more or less likely. In addition, individualized assessments which take account of the specific contexts and circumstances of different people's lives will help to ensure that any subsequent actions or interventions appropriately reflect the diversity of individuals and communities.

In a climate of limited resources, not all cases can have equal 'thinking time' and some assessments will need to be more detailed than others, but it is important to be alert to elements of risk in all situations and decisions. In each case, there needs to be an understanding of:

• the skills required to exercise sound judgement and make good decisions about risk;
• the emotions, values, attitudes and biases that can affect decision making in negative ways.

*What does this mean?* is perhaps the most critical question we can ask of information we receive. The second is perhaps *what should I now do in the light of this information?* Earlier chapters have highlighted the need to carefully consider the reliability of information before deciding how much weight to attach to it. Chapter 3 also illustrated some of the biases that can affect our decision making, such as the tendency to place too much emphasis on first impressions and to ignore information which suggests that those initial ideas might need to be revised.

It was suggested that one helpful way to look at risk assessment is to view initial judgements as *hypotheses* which need to be robustly tested and updated where necessary. Alternative ways of making decisions, such as rehearsing risk scenarios, can also assist practitioners to weigh up options more explicitly, to rehearse possible consequences of their decisions and to consider contingency actions that might be required to manage any changes in risk. Gaps in knowledge and resources mean that professional judgements are often necessarily limited, but we can guard against this by being critically reflective about our decisions and continually alert to the need to review assessments in light of the dynamic nature of risk.

## Responding to Risk

'[T]he aim of assessment is to guide action' (Reder, Duncan and Gray 1993: 83) and this links to the second key question above, i.e. *what should I now do in the light of this information?* Risk assessment has to lead to appropriate and proportional risk management. This should seek to reduce the likelihood of harmful outcomes occurring or, if they do occur, reducing the degree of harm that will be caused. As noted in chapter 2, however, effective work with people doesn't just involve the avoidance of risk, but also requires the taking of positive risks to support personal growth and development. This is one of the many balances that have to be taken into account when working with risk, and the complexities of balancing competing sets of needs, rights and responsibilities have been explored in discussions throughout the book.

---

### Activity 8.1   Achieving 'Balanced' Practice

Identify two or three situations where you have had to make (or seen others make) difficult decisions about risk.

Bearing in mind that 'balance' does not mean weighting each element equally, but having an *appropriate* balance for the specific situation, how did each of these decisions:

- balance negative and positive risks?
- balance risk, needs and rights?
- balance the decision maker's responsibilities and the responsibilities of others?

The balance will vary in different cases. In your examples, what were the reasons for this and were the differences appropriate?

Risk-management plans should be specific about the changes that need to be made to achieve both harm reduction and positive outcomes. The areas for intervention that are chosen need to be those most likely to make a difference to outcomes, with careful consideration given to the most appropriate timing for specific interventions. In some cases, for example, effective preventative action at an earlier stage would avoid the need for more intrusive intervention once risk has escalated. Plans need to have clear goals and the smaller steps necessary to achieve these aims should be planned out in advance in a way that is realistic. In addition, plans are likely to require a range of complementary strategies and also need to be flexible to take account of changing circumstances.

Risk assessment and risk management require working with others, both within a particular agency and across different organizations. Plans need to clearly set out the roles and responsibilities of everyone involved and each individual has a responsibility to ensure that they communicate effectively with others in managing a case. Priority should also be given to involving service users in the process where appropriate and encouraging them to 'own' the risk-management plan (to some degree at least). This active involvement is important because it can help people to feel that they can contribute to decision making, so that interventions are more relevant to their individual circumstances.

Risk assessment is an ongoing process and requires the identification of patterns of behaviour over time. Keeping accurate and detailed records is therefore an important part of the process. These need to be actively used, however – not just filed away – to help ensure that any changes over time or new information that comes to light can inform the continuing assessment of risk. Practitioners also need to regularly reflect on risk-management plans to check that the actions being taken are still relevant and that they contribute to achieving the desired outcomes.

## Working Positively with the Challenges of Risk: A Shared Commitment

Risk assessment and risk management inevitably present many ethical dilemmas for practitioners and these were explored in chapter 5. They included: the tension between care and control issues; the difficulty of balancing conflicting rights (for example, between children and parents); issues surrounding the compulsory detention of persons with a mental disorder; and the challenge of balancing the need to protect adults from self-harm, while also recognizing their right to make choices about their own lives. Such ethical dilemmas are an intrinsic part of social work practice and need to be faced positively rather than feared: thinking ahead is important so as not to be taken by surprise when difficult questions arise.

Professional standards provide a framework for practice and these will generally indicate that practitioners should aim to protect and enhance the rights, choices and autonomy of service users unless 'required by law to protect that person or another from risk of serious harm' (BASW 2012b: 12). However, no framework can cover all possible scenarios. Neither does this book attempt to provide all the answers. Instead, there has been an emphasis throughout on the need for critical reflection and the importance of weighing up different options when considering solutions to the ethical challenges of daily practice.

Critical reflection is a task required of individuals, but it also needs to be a central element of organizational responses to risk. Professional knowledge needs to be applied with skill, discretion and expertise within the defined boundaries of organizational policies and procedures. Chapter 6 considered the critical role of 'risk controllers' in ensuring that risk systems are both fit for purpose and facilitate thoughtful practice by staff. If practitioners are to make good risk decisions, they need the support of managers and a working culture focused on improving practice. This includes learning the lessons from serious incidents – with the need to improve communication between professionals being one of the key recurring themes – and being willing to ask challenging questions about the practice of individual teams or departments. While the fault for practice failings can sometimes lie with individual practitioners, it will at other times be due to weaknesses in organizational procedures. Managers need to ensure therefore that they have effective oversight of risk systems.

Developing high-quality risk-assessment and risk-management practice requires a shared commitment from individual practitioners and social work organizations. As well as learning from problems or mistakes, sharing good practice should also be a priority. The aim should be to work towards a practice culture in which individual practitioners strive to keep on learning, and where managers actively help staff to review their practice and identify how they might improve their risk-assessment and risk-management work.

This approach to practice moves from a blaming culture to a learning culture, and can be one of the most significant drivers for improving practice and achieving better outcomes for service users and the wider community. A learning culture is one way in which the inevitable pressure that is part of social work can be managed, both individually and collectively, so as to avoid the negative outcomes that may occur when too much stress adversely affects practitioner performance. The challenge therefore is for staff to find ways to operate at their best, given the inherent difficulties of their working environment, and once again this requires a shared commitment from both individual practitioners and managers of social work organizations.

Individuals will operate most effectively if they have developed self-management and coping skills and, as discussed in chapter 7, this can involve both problem-solving and emotion-focused coping. The critical thinking skills highlighted throughout this book need to be applied not just to analysing the quality of risk decisions but also to reflecting on one's emotional and cognitive responses to difficult situations and the implications of these reactions for decision making. There needs to be a balance between emotional engagement with service users and maintaining some distance and perspective so as to avoid burn-out. A key sign of professional maturity – but one that is often overlooked – is knowing how to ask for help and support when necessary. In return, organizations should pay attention to how workplaces can be structured to minimize unhelpful stress and to make the most of staff skills and abilities. Particular focus should be given to the supervisory relationship which should provide a balance between holding practitioners to account and promoting learning. Individuals who receive this kind of balanced supervision will have the security of clear boundaries and expectations, but also the chance to develop as critical and reflective practitioners. As part of that process, the final activity below prompts you to reflect on how your practice, whatever your organizational role, could develop as a result of what you've read here.

---

**Activity 8.2 Reflection**

Based on your reading of this book, consider:

- what you have learned that has been new;
- how this will affect the next piece of work around risk that you take on;
- what other learning or training could help you to work more effectively with risk.

The balance will vary in different cases. In your examples, what were the reasons for this and were the differences appropriate?

---

# References

Adams, J. (1995) *Risk*. London: UCL Press.

Appleton, J. and Oates, J. (2010) *Collaborative Working with Children's Centres: A Research and Development Project*. Milton Keynes PCT and DoH, Collaborative Study with Open University.

Baker, K. (2005) 'Assessment in youth justice: professional discretion and the use of *Asset*', *Youth Justice* 5: 106–22.

Baker, K. (2007) 'Risk in practice: systems and practitioner judgement', in M. Blyth, E. Solomon and K. Baker (eds), *Young People and Risk*. Bristol: Policy Press.

Baker, K. and Wilkinson, B. (2011) 'Professional risk taking and defensible decisions', in H. Kemshall and B. Wilkinson (eds), *Good Practice in Assessing Risk: Current Knowledge, Issues and Approaches*. London: Jessica Kingsley.

Baker, K., Kelly, G. and Wilkinson, B. (2011) *Assessment in Youth Justice*. Bristol: Policy Press.

Balen, R. and Masson, H. (2008) 'The Victoria Climbié case: social work education for practice in children and families' work before and since', *Child and Family Social Work* 13: 121–32.

Bandura, A. (2007) *Self-Efficacy: The Exercise of Self-Control*. New York: Freeman.

Banks, S. (2009) 'Integrity in professional life: issues of conduct, commitment and capacity', *British Journal of Social Work* 40: 2168–84.

Banks, S. (2011) 'Ethics in an age of austerity: social work and the evolving public management', *Journal of Social Intervention: Theory and Practice* 20: 5–23.

Banks, S. (2012) *Ethics and Values in Social Work*, 4th edn. Basingstoke: Palgrave Macmillan.

Barach, P. and Small, S. (2000) 'Reporting and preventing medical mishaps: lessons from non-medical near miss reporting systems', *British Medical Journal* 320(7237): 759–63.

Barker, J. and Hodes, D. (2007) *The Child in Mind: A Child Protection Handbook*, 3rd edn. Abingdon: Routledge.

Barnett, G. and Mann, R. (2011) 'Good lives and risk assessment: collaborative approaches to risk assessment with sexual offenders', in H. Kemshall and B. Wilkinson (eds), *Good Practice in Assessing Risk: Current Knowledge, Issues and Approaches*. London: Jessica Kingsley.

Barry, E. (2009) 'An examination of ethics in social work', *Critical Social Thinking: Policy and Practice* 1: 110–24.

BASW (2012a) 'The Code Makers', available at: http://cdn.basw.co.uk/upload/basw_21546-9.pdf, accessed 2 March 2013.

BASW (2012b) *The Code of Ethics for Social Work: Statement of Principles*. Available at: http://cdn.basw.co.uk/upload/basw_112315-7.pdf, accessed 2 March 2013.

BBC News (2010) 'Little Ted's was "ideal" place for Vanessa George abuse', www.bbc.co.uk/news/uk-england-devon-11682161, accessed 1 March 2013.

BBC News (2011) 'Catholic bishop orders South West child protection review', 28 October, www.bbc.co.uk/news/uk-england-devon-15491833, accessed 1 March 2013.

Beckett, C. (2008) 'Risk uncertainty and thresholds', in M. Calder (ed.), *Contemporary Risk Assessment in Safeguarding Children*. Lyme Regis: Russell House Publishing, pp. 40–51.

Beddoe, L. (2010) 'Surveillance or reflection: professional supervision in the risk society', *British Journal of Social Work* 40: 1297–1313.

Beech, A. and Mann, R. (2002) 'Recent developments in the successful treatment of sex offenders', in J. McGuire (ed.), *Offender Rehabilitation and Treatment*. Chichester: Wiley, pp. 259–88.

Bibby, P. (1994) *Personal Safety for Social Workers*. Aldershot: Arena.

Bissell, G. (2012) *Organisational Behaviour for Social Work*. Bristol: Policy Press.

Blom-Cooper, L., Hally, H. and Murphy, E. (1995) *The Falling Shadow: One Patient's Mental Health Care*. London: Duckworth.

Boeck, T. and Fleming, J. (2011) 'The role of social capital and resources in resilience to risk', in H. Kemshall and B. Wilkinson (eds), *Good Practice in Assessing Risk: Current Knowledge, Issues and Approaches*. London: Jessica Kingsley, pp. 48–65.

Bornat, J. and Bytheway, B. (2010) 'Perceptions and presentations of living with everyday risk in later life', *British Journal of Social Work* 40: 1118–34.

Bostock, L., Bairstow, S., Fish, S. and MacLeod, F. (2005) *Managing Risk and Minimising Mistakes in Services to Children and Families*. London: Social Care Institute for Excellence.

Bowes, A., Avan, G. and Macintosh, S. (2008) 'Elder abuse and black and minority ethnic communities: lessons for good practice', in J. Pritchard (ed.), *Good Practice in Safeguarding Adults: Working Effectively in Adult Protection.* London: Jessica Kingsley, pp. 83–100.

Brandon, M., Dodsworth, J. and Rumball, D. (2005) 'Serious case reviews: learning to use expertise', *Child Abuse Review* 14: 160–76.

Brandon, M., Belderson, P., Warren, C. et al. (2008a) 'The preoccupation with thresholds in cases of child death or serious injury through abuse and neglect', *Child Abuse Review* 17: 313–30.

Brandon, M., Belderson, P., Warren, C. et al. (2008b) *Analysing Child Deaths and Serious Injuries through Abuse and Neglect: What Can We Learn?* London: DCFS.

Brandon, M., Bailey, S., Belderson, P. et al. (2009) *Understanding Serious Case Reviews and their Impact.* London: Department for Children, Schools and Families.

Brandon, M., Bailey, S. and Belderson, P. (2010) *Building on the Learning from Serious Case Reviews: A Two Year Analysis of Child Protection Database Notifications 2007–2009.* London: Department for Education.

Broadhurst, K., Hall, C., Wastell, D., White, S. and Pithouse, A. (2010) 'Risk instrumentalism and the humane project in social work: identifying the informal logics of risk management in children's statutory services', *British Journal of Social Work* 40: 1046–64.

Burton, J. and Van den Broeck, D. (2009) 'Accountable and countable: information management systems and the bureaucratisation of social work', *British Journal of Social Work* 39: 1326–42.

Calder, M. (2008a) 'Organisational dangerousness: causes, consequences and correctives', in M. Calder (ed.), *Contemporary Risk Assessment in Safeguarding Children.* Lyme Regis: Russell House Publishing, pp. 119–65.

Calder, M. (2008b) 'Professional dangerousness: causes and contemporary features', in M. Calder (ed.), *Contemporary Risk Assessment in Safeguarding Children.* Lyme Regis: Russell House Publishing, pp. 61–96.

Calder, M. (2011) 'Organisationally dangerous practice: political drivers, practice implications and pathways to resolution', in H. Kemshall and B. Wilkinson (eds), *Good Practice in Assessing Risk: Current Issues, Knowledge and Approaches.* London: Jessica Kingsley, pp. 195–213.

Callaghan, D., Kelly, G. and Wilkinson, B. (2009) *The Jigsaw Approach: A Programme for Young People in the Community.* Manchester: Youth Justice Services and KWP.

Cambridge, P. (2004) 'Abuse inquiries as learning tools for social care organisations', in J. Manthorpe and N. Stanley (eds), *The Age of the Inquiry.* London: Routledge, pp. 231–54.

Carey, M. and Foster, V. (2011) 'Introducing "deviant" social work: contextualising the limits of radical social work whilst understanding (fragmented) resistance within the social work labour process', *British Journal of Social Work* 41: 576–93.

Carlile, Lord (2012) *Doncaster: Carlile Independent Review*. London: Department for Education.

Carr, S. (2010) *Enabling Risk, Securing Safety: Self-directed Support and Personal Budgets*. London: SCIE.

Carson, D. (1996) 'Risking legal repercussions', in H. Kemshall and J. Pritchard (eds), *Good Practice in Risk Assessment and Risk Management*, vol. 1. London: Jessica Kingsley Publishers, pp. 3–12.

Carson, D. and Bain, A. (2008) *Professional Risk and Working with People*. London: Jessica Kingsley Publishers.

Children's Workforce Development Council (2010) *Common Core of Skills and Knowledge: At the Heart of What You Do*. London: DCSF.

Clarke, J. (2006) Impact issues for treatment providers: challenging assumptions. Presentation to NOTA conference. Unpublished.

Clarke, J. (2008) 'Promoting professional resilience', in M. Calder (ed.), *Contemporary Risk Assessment in Safeguarding Children*. Lyme Regis: Russell House Publishing, pp. 166–84.

Coffey, M., Dugdill, L. and Tattersall, A. (2004) 'Research note: stress in social services: Mental well-being, constraints and job satisfaction', *British Journal of Social Work* 34: 735–47.

Collins, S. (2008) 'Statutory social workers: stress, job satisfaction, coping, social support and individual differences', *British Journal of Social Work* 38: 1173–93.

COMEST (2005) *The Precautionary Principle*. Paris: UNESCO.

Cooperrider, D., Whitney, D. and Stavros, J. (2008) *Appreciative Inquiry Handbook*, 2nd edn. Brunswick: Crown Custom Publishing.

Corby, B. (2000) *Child Abuse: Towards a Knowledge Base*, 2nd edn. Maidenhead: Open University Press.

Craft, C. (n.d.) 'Child abuse risk factors: contributing to emotional abuse and neglect', http://adoption.about.com/od/parenting/a/childabuserisks.htm, accessed 2 March 2013.

Craissati, J. and Sindall, O. (2009) 'Serious further offences: an exploration of risk and typologies', *Probation Journal* 56: 9–27.

Darlington, Y., Healy, K. and Feeney, J. A. (2010) 'Challenges in implementing participatory practice in child protection: a contingency approach', *Children and Youth Service Review* 32: 1020–7.

Daston, L. (1987) 'The domestication of risk: mathematical probability and insurance 1650–1830', in L. Krueger, L. Daston and M. Heidelberger (eds), *The Probabilistic Revolution, vol. 1: Ideas in History*. Cambridge, MA: MIT Press.

Davidson-Arad, B. (2010) 'Four perspectives on the quality of life of children at risk kept at home and removed from home in Israel', *British Journal of Social Work* 40: 1719–35.

Davies, L. (2008) 'Reclaiming the language of child protection', in M. Calder (ed.), *Contemporary Risk Assessment in Safeguarding Children*. Lyme Regis: Russell House Publishing, pp. 25–39.

Debidin, M. (ed.) (2009) *A Compendium of Research and Analysis on the Offender Assessment System (OASys) 2006–2009*. London: Ministry of Justice.

Denney, D. (2005) *Risk and Society*. London: Sage.

Denney, D. (2010) 'Violence and social care staff: positive and negative approaches to risk', *British Journal of Social Work* 40: 1297–1313.

Department for Children, Schools and Families (2008) *Information Sharing Guidance for Practitioners and Managers*. London: DCSF.

Department for Children, Schools and Families (2010) *Working Together to Safeguard Children: A Guide to Inter-Agency Working to Safeguard and Promote the Welfare of Children*. London: DCSF.

Department for Constitutional Affairs (2006) *Review of the Implementation of the Human Rights Act*, available at: www.conorgearty.co.uk/pdfs/HRAfull_review.pdf, accessed 1 March 2013.

Department for Education (2011) *An Action Plan for Adoption: Tackling Delays*. London: DfE.

Department of Health (2000) *An Organisation with a Memory: Report of an Expert Group on Learning from Adverse Events in the NHS*. London: Department of Health.

Department of Health (2005) *Independent Investigation of Adverse Events in Mental Health Services*. London: DoH.

Department of Health (2007) *Independence, Choice and Risk: A Guide to Best Practice in Supported Decision Making*. London: DoH.

Department of Health and Social Security (1975) *Report of the Committee on Inquiry into the Provision and Co-ordination of Services to the Family of John George Aukland*. London: HMSO.

Devaney, J. (2008) 'Chronic child abuse and domestic violence: children and families with long-term and complex needs', *Child and Family Social Work* 13: 443–53.

Dolgoff, R., Harrington, D. and Loewenberg, F. (2011) *Ethical Decisions for Social Work Practice*. Belmont, CA: Brooks Cole.

Donnellan, H. and Jack, G. (2010) *The Survival Guide for Newly Qualified Social Workers: Hitting the Ground Running*. London: Jessica Kingsley.

Donnelly, E. and Neville, L. (2008) *Communication and Inter-Personal Skills*. Newton Abbott: Reflect Press.

Downham, G. and Lingham, R. (2009) 'Learning lessons: using inquiries for change', *Journal of Mental Health Law* 57: 57–69.

Driscoll, J. (2009) 'Prevalence, people and processes: a consideration of the implications of Lord Laming's progress report on the protection of children in England', *Child Abuse Review* 18: 333–45.

Dryden-Edwards, R. and Stöppler, M. C. (n.d.) 'Domestic abuse', www.emedicinehealth.com/domestic_violence/page3_cm.htm, accessed 3 March 2013.

Eadie, T. and Canton, R. (2002) 'Practising in a context of ambivalence: the challenge for youth justice workers', *Youth Justice* 2: 14–26.

Edwards, A., Daniels, H., Gallagher, T. et al. (2009) *Improving Inter-Professional Collaborations: Multi-Agency Working for Children's Well-Being*. London: Routledge.

Elwyn, G., Edwards, A., Eccles, M. and Rovner, D. (2001) 'Decision analysis in patient care', *The Lancet* 358(9281) (Aug 2001): 571–4.

Ericson, R. (2007) 'A review article of Magnus Hornqvist, *The Organised Nature of Power: On Productive and Repressive Based on Consideration of Risk*', *British Journal of Criminology* 47: 955–68.

Evans, T. and Hardy, M. (2010) *Evidence & Knowledge for Practice: Skills for Contemporary Social Work*. Cambridge: Polity Press.

Evans, T. and Harris, J. (2004) 'Street-level bureaucracy, social work and the (exaggerated) death of discretion', *British Journal of Social Work* 34: 871–95.

Evans, A., Roberts, K., Price, H. and Stefek, C. (2010) 'The use of paraphrasing in investigative interviews', *Child Abuse and Neglect* 34: 585–92.

Farmer, E., Sturgess, W. and O'Neill, T. (2008) *Reunion of Looked After Children with their Parents: Patterns, Interventions and Outcomes*. London: DCSF.

Farnham, F. and James, D. (2001) ' "Dangerousness" and dangerous law', *The Lancet* 358(9297): 1926.

Farrow, K., Kelly, G. and Wilkinson, B. (2007) *Offenders in Focus: Risk, Responsivity and Diversity*. Bristol: The Policy Press.

Ferguson, H. (2010) 'Walks, home visits and atmospheres: risk and the everyday practices and motilities of social work and child protection', *British Journal of Social Work* 40: 1100–17.

Fish, S. (2009) *What are the Key Questions for Audit of Child Protection Systems and Decision-Making?* London: Centre for Excellence and Outcomes in Children and Young People's Services (C4EO).

Fish, S., Munro, E. and Bairstow, S. (2008) *Learning Together to Safeguard Children: Developing a Multi-Agency Systems Approach for Case Reviews*. London: Social Care Institute for Excellence.

Forrester, D., Kershaw, S., Moss, H. and Hughes, L. (2008a) 'Communication skills in child protection: how do social workers talk to parents?', *Child and Family Social Work* 13: 41–51.

Forrester, D., McCambridge, J., Waissbein, C. and Rollnick, S. (2008b) 'How did child and family social workers talk to parents about child welfare concerns?', *Child Abuse Review* 17: 23–35.

France, A., Freiberg, K. and Homel, R. (2010) 'Beyond risk factors: towards a holistic prevention paradigm for children and young people', *British Journal of Social Work* 40: 1192–1210.

Francis, R. Q. C. (2006) *Report of the Independent Inquiry into the Care and Treatment of Michael Stone*. Kent County Council, Kent Probation Area: South East Coast Strategic Health Authority.

Gardner, D. (2008) *Risk: The Science and Politics of Fear*. London: Virgin Books.

Gilbert, T. (2009) 'A comparison of the International Statement of Principles in Social Work with the Code of Ethics for British Social Workers', *The Journal of Social Work Values and Ethics* 6(2), available online at: www.socialworker.com/jswve/content/view/121/68/; accessed 1 March 2013.

Gilovich, T., Griffin, D. and Kahneman, D. (2002) *Heuristics and Biases: The Psychology of Intuitive Judgement*. Cambridge: Cambridge University Press.

Goddard, C. and Tucci, J. (1991) 'Child protection and the need for the reappraisal of the social worker–client relationship', *Australian Social Work* 44: 3–10.

Goldstein, W. and Hogarth, R. (eds) (1997) *Research on Judgement and Decision Making: Currents, Connections and Controversies (Cambridge Series on Judgement and Decision Making)*. Cambridge: Cambridge University Press.

Goleman, D. (1996) *Emotional Intelligence: Why It Can Matter More than IQ*. London: Bloomsbury.

Gove, M. (2012) *Letter from the Education Secretary on the Publication of the Edlington SCR*. London: Department for Education.

Greene, E. and Ellis, L. (2007) 'Decision making in criminal justice', in D. Carson, B. Milne, F. Pakes, K. Shalev and A. Shawyer (eds), *Applying Psychology to Criminal Justice*. Chichester: Wiley, pp. 183–200.

Hacking, I. (1987) 'Was there a probabilistic revolution 1800–1930?', in L. Krueger, L. Daston and M. Heidelberger (eds), *The Probabilistic Revolution, vol. 1: Ideas in History*. Cambridge, MA: MIT Press.

Hacking, I. (1990) *The Taming of Chance*. Cambridge: Cambridge University Press.

Hall, C. and Slembrouck, S. (2009) 'Professional categorization, risk management and inter-agency communication in public inquiries into disastrous outcomes', *British Journal of Social Work* 39: 280–98.

Hammond, K. (1996) *Human Judgement and Social Policy*. Oxford: Oxford University Press.

Haringey LSCB (2009) *Serious Case Review Baby Peter: Executive Summary*. London: Haringey LSCB.

Harvard Mental Health Letter (2011) 'Mental illness and violence', www.health.harvard.edu/newsletters/Harvard_Mental_Health_Letter/2011/January/mental-illness-and-violence, accessed 2 March 2013.

Heilbrun, K. and Erikson, J. (2007) 'A behavioural science perspective on identifying and managing hindsight bias and unstructured judgement: implications for legal decision making', in D. Carson, B. Milne, F. Pakes, K. Shalev and A. Shawyer (eds), *Applying Psychology to Criminal Justice*. Chichester: Wiley, pp. 201–10.

Higgs, H. (ed.) (1931) *Richard Cantillon: Essay on the Nature of Commerce in General*. London: Home Office.

Hill, A. (2010) *Working in Statutory Contexts*. Cambridge: Polity Press.

HM Inspectorate of Probation (2009) *Public Protection and Safeguarding – An Inspectorate Perspective*. London: Her Majesty's Inspectorate of Probation.

Hollomotz, A. (2009) 'Beyond "vulnerability": an ecological model approach to conceptualizing risk of sexual violence against people with learning difficulties', *British Journal of Social Work* 39: 99–112.

Hollows, A. (2008) 'Professional judgement and the risk assessment process', in M. Calder (ed.), *Contemporary Risk Assessment in Safeguarding Children*. Lyme Regis: Russell House Publishing, pp. 52–60.

Home Education Forums (n.d.) 'Putting professional child abusers on the map', http://www.home-education.biz/news/23/60/Putting-professional-child-abusers-on-the-map/, accessed 1 March 2013.

Home Office and Department of Health (1999) *Managing Dangerous People with Severe Personality Disorder – Proposals for Policy Development*. London: Home Office and Department of Health.

Hothersall, S. and Maas-Lowitt, M. (2010) *Need, Risk and Protection in Social Work Practice*. Exeter: Learning Matters.

Hough, M. (1996) *Drug Misuse and the Criminal Justice System: A Review of the Literature*. Drug Prevention Initiative, Paper 15, London: Home Office.

Howe, D. (2008) *The Emotionally Intelligent Social Worker*. Basingstoke: Palgrave Macmillan.

Hugman, R. (2005) *New Approaches in Ethics for the Caring Professions*. New York: Palgrave Macmillan.

Hugman, R. (2008) 'An ethical perspective on social work', in M. Davies (ed.), *The Blackwell Companion to Social Work*, 3rd edn. Oxford: Blackwell.

Institute of Medicine (1999) *To Err is Human: Building a Safer Health System*. Washington, DC: National Academic Press.

International Federation of Social Workers, The (IFSW) 'Code of ethics'. Available at: http://ifsw.org/policies/code-of-ethics/, accessed 27 February 2013.

Juhila, K. (2009) 'From care to fellowship and back: interpretive repertoires used by the social welfare workers when describing their relationship with homeless women', *British Journal of Social Work* 39: 128–43.

Kahneman, D., Slovic, P. and Tversky, A. (1990) *Judgements under Uncertainty: Heuristics and Biases*. Cambridge: Cambridge University Press.

Kemshall, H. (1997a) *The Management and Assessment of Risk: Training Pack*. London: Home Office.

Kemshall, H. (1997b) 'Sleep safely: crime risks may be smaller than you think', *Social Policy and Administration* 31: 246–60.

Kemshall, H. (1998a) 'Defensible decisions for risk: or "it's the doers wot get the blame"', *Probation Journal* 45: 67–72.

Kemshall, H. (1998b) *Risk in Probation Practice*. Aldershot: Ashgate.

Kemshall, H. (2002a) 'Risk assessment and management', in M. Davies (ed.), *The Blackwell Companion to Social Work*. Oxford: Blackwell Publishing.

Kemshall, H. (2002b) *Risk, Social Policy and Welfare*. Maidenhead: McGraw Hill and Open University Press.

Kemshall, H. (2003) *Understanding Risk in Criminal Justice*. Maidenhead: Open University Press.

Kemshall, H. (2008a) 'Risks, rights and justice: understanding and responding to youth risk', *Youth Justice* 8: 21–37.

Kemshall, H. (2008b) 'Actuarial and clinical risk assessment: contrasts, comparisons and collective usages', in M. Calder (ed.), *Contemporary Risk Assessment in Safeguarding Children*. Lyme Regis: Russell House Publishing, pp. 198–205.

Kemshall, H. (2008c) *Understanding the Community Management of High Risk Offenders*. Maidenhead: McGraw Hill/Open University Press.

Kemshall, H. (2010a) 'Risk rationalities in contemporary social work policy and practice', *British Journal of Social Work* 40: 1247–62.

Kemshall, H. (2010b) 'The role of risk, needs and strengths assessment in improving the supervision of offenders', in F. McNeill, P. Raynor and C. Trotter (eds), *Offender Supervision: New Directions in Theory, Research and Practice*. Cullompton: Willan.

Kemshall, H. and Wilkinson, B. (2011) (eds) *Good Practice in Assessing Risk: Current Knowledge, Issues and Approaches*. London: Jessica Kingsley.

Kemshall, H. and Wood, J. (2007) 'Beyond public protection', *Criminology and Criminal Justice* 7: 203–22.

Kemshall, H. and Wood, J. (2008) 'Risk and public protection: responding to involuntary and taboo risk', *Social Policy and Administration* 42: 611–29.

Kemshall, H., Mackenzie, G., Miller, J. and Wilkinson, B. (2011) *Risk of Harm Guidance and Training Resource*. Leicester: De Montfort University and London: National Offender Management Service.

Keys, M. (2009a) 'Determining the skills for child protection practice: From quandary to quagmire', *Child Abuse Review* 18: 297–315.

Keys, M. (2009b) 'Determining the skills for child protection practice: Emerging from the quagmire!', *Child Abuse Review* 18: 316–32.

Kida, T. (2006) *Don't Believe Everything You Think: The Six Basic Mistakes We Make in Thinking*. New York: Prometheus Books.

Kitzinger, J. (2004) *Framing Abuse: Media Influence and Public Understanding of Sexual Violence against Children*. London: Pluto Press.

Klein, G. (1999) *Sources of Power: How People Make Decisions*. Cambridge, MA: MIT Press.

Koprowska, J. (2010) *Communication and Interpersonal Skills in Social Work*. Exeter: Learning Matters.

Laming, H. (2003) *The Victoria Climbié Inquiry: Report of an Inquiry by Lord Laming*. London: The Stationery Office.

Laming, H. (2009) *The Protection of Children in England: A Progress Report*. London: House of Commons.

Langan, J. (2009) 'Mental health, risk communication and data quality in the electronic age', *British Journal of Social Work* 39: 467–87.

Lehrer, J. (2009) *The Decision Moment: How the Brain Makes up its Mind*. New York: Canongate.

Leighton, N. (1985) 'Personal and professional values – marriage or divorce?', in D. Watson (ed.), *A Code of Ethics for Social Work*. London: Routledge.

Lichtenstein, S. and Slovic, P. (eds) (2006) *The Construction of Preference*. Cambridge: Cambridge University Press.

Littlechild, R. and Glasby, J. (2011) 'Risk and personalisation', in H. Kemshall and B. Wilkinson (eds), *Good Practice in Assessing Risk: Current Knowledge, Issues and Approaches*. London: Jessica Kingsley Publishers, pp. 155–73.

London Borough of Brent (1985) *A Child in Trust: The Report of the Panel of Inquiry into the Circumstances Surrounding the Death of Jasmine Beckford*. London: London Borough of Brent.

Loughton, T. (2010) *Publication of Serious Case Review Overview Reports and Munro Review of Child Protection (Letter to LSCB Chairs and Directors of Children's Services)*. London: Department for Education.

Macdonald, G. and Macdonald, K. (2010) 'Safeguarding: a case for intelligent risk management', *British Journal of Social Work* 40: 1174–91.

Maden, T. (2011) 'Mental health and risk', in H. Kemshall and B. Wilkinson (eds), *Good Practice in Assessing Risk: Current Knowledge, Issues and Approaches*. London: Jessica Kingsley, pp. 102–18.

Manthorpe, J. and Moriarty, J. (2010) *Nothing Ventured, Nothing Gained: Risk Guidance for People with Dementia*. London: DoH.

Manthorpe, J., Kharicha, K., Goodman, C. et al. (2010) 'Smarter working in social and health care: professional perspectives on a new technology for risk appraisal with older people', *British Journal of Social Work* 40: 1829–46.

Martin, K. and Jeffes, J. (2011) *Safeguarding Children Peer Review Programme: Learning and Recommendations*. Slough: NFER.

Maruna, S. and Mann, R. (2006) 'A fundamental attribution error? Rethinking cognitive distortions?', *Legal and Criminal Psychology* 11: 155–77.

McDonald, A. (2010a) *Social Work with Older People*. Cambridge: Polity Press.

McDonald, A. (2010b) 'The impact of the 2005 Mental Capacity Act on social workers' decision making and approaches to the assessment of risk', *British Journal of Social Work* 40: 1229–46.

McGaw, S., Scully, T. and Pritchard, C. (2010) 'Predicting the unpredictable? Identifying high-risk versus low-risk parents with intellectual disabilities', *Child Abuse and Neglect* 34: 699–710.

McGrath, M. and Oyebode, F. (2002) 'Qualitative analysis of recommendations in 79 inquiries after homicide committed by persons with mental illness', *Journal of Mental Health Law* (December): 262–82.

Mills, C. and Vine, P. (1990) 'Critical incident reporting – an approach to reviewing the investigation and management of child abuse', *British Journal of Social Work* 20: 215–20.

Milner, J. and O'Byrne, P. (2009) *Assessment in Social Work*, 3rd edn. Basingstoke: Palgrave Macmillan.

Moore, B. (1996) *Risk Assessment: A Practitioner's Guide to Predicting Harmful Behaviour*. London: Whiting and Birch.

Morrison, T. (2007) 'Emotional intelligence, emotion and social work: context, characteristics, complications and contribution', *British Journal of Social Work* 37: 245–63.

Munro, E. (1995) 'The power of first impressions', *Practice* 7: 59–65.

Munro, E. (1996) 'Avoidable and unavoidable mistakes in child protection work', *British Journal of Social Work* 26: 793–808.

Munro, E. (1998) *Understanding Social Work: An Empirical Approach*. London: Athlone Press.

Munro, E. (1999) 'Common errors of reasoning in child protection work', *Child Abuse and Neglect* 23: 745–58.

Munro, E. (2007) *Child Protection*. London: Sage.

Munro, E. (2008a) *Effective Child Protection*, 2nd edn. London: Sage.

Munro, E. (2008b) 'Lessons learnt, boxes ticked, families ignored', *The Independent*, 16 November, www.independent.co.uk/voices/commentators/eileen-munro-lessons-learnt-boxes-ticked-families-ignored-1020508.html, accessed 1 March 2013.

Munro, E. (2010a) 'Learning to reduce risk in child protection', *British Journal of Social Work* 40: 1135–51.

Munro, E. (2010b) 'Conflating risks: implications for accurate risk prediction in child welfare services', *Health, Risk and Society* 12: 119–30.

Munro, E. (2010c) *The Munro Review of Child Protection, Part One: A Systems Perspective*. London: Department for Education.

Munro, E. (2011) *The Munro Review of Child Protection Final Report: A Child-Centred System*. London: Department for Education.

Nash, M. (2010) 'Singing from the same MAPPA hymn sheet – but can we hear all the voices?', in A. Pycroft and D. Gough (eds), *Multi-agency Working in Criminal Justice*. Bristol: The Policy Press, pp. 111–22.

National Confidential Inquiry into Suicide and Homicide by People with Mental Illness (2010) *Independent Investigations after Homicide by People Receiving Mental Health Care*. Manchester: Centre for Suicide Prevention.

National Council on Independent Living (NCIL) (1999) *Government White Paper: Modernising Social Services – Response by the British Council of Disabled People's National Centre for Independent Living*. London: NCIL.

National Patient Safety Agency (2008) *Independent Investigation of Serious Patient Safety Incidents in Mental Health Services: Good Practice Guidance*. London: NPSA.

NHS London (2006) *Report of the Independent Inquiry into the Care and Treatment of John Barrett*. London: NHS.

Noble, C. and Irwin, J. (2009) 'Social work supervision: an exploration of the current challenges in a rapidly changing social, economic and political environment', *Journal of Social Work* 9: 345–58.

Nolen-Hoeksema, S., Wisco, B. and Lyubomosicsky, S. (2008) 'Rethinking rumination', *Perspectives on Psychological Science* 3: 400–24.

Ofsted (2011) *Ages of Concern: Learning Lessons from Serious Case Reviews*. Manchester: Ofsted.

O'Rourke, L. (2010) *Recording in Social Work*. Bristol: The Policy Press.

Osmond, J. and O'Connor, I. (2004) 'Formalizing the unformalized: practitioners' communication of knowledge in practice', *British Journal of Social Work* 34: 677–92.

*Oxford English Dictionary* (2012) Oxford: Oxford University Press. Available at: www.oed.com/; accessed 28 February 2013.

Parker, J. and Bradley, G. (2007) *Social Work Practice: Assessment, Planning, Intervention and Review*. Exeter: Learning Matters.

Paul, R. and Elder, L. (2006) *The Miniature Guide to Critical Thinking: Concepts and Tools*. Dillon Beach, CA: Foundation for Critical Thinking.

Peay, J. (1996) *Inquiries after Homicide*. London: Duckworth.

Peckover, S., Broadhurst, K., White, S. et al. (2011) 'The fallacy of formulation: practice makes process in the assessment of risk to children', in H. Kemshall and B. Wilkinson (eds), *Good Practice in Assessing Risk: Current Knowledge, Issues and Approaches*. London: Jessica Kingsley Publishers, pp. 84–101.

Pidgeon, N., Kasperson, R. and Slovic, P. (2003) *The Social Amplification of Risk*. Cambridge: Cambridge University Press.

Pithouse, A., Hall, C., Peckover, S. and White, S. (2009) 'A tale of two CAFs: The impact of the electronic common assessment framework', *British Journal of Social Work* 39: 599–612.

Plous, S. (1993) *The Psychology of Judgement and Decision Making*. Philadelphia, PA: Temple University Press.

Power, M. (2004) *The Risk Management of Everything: Rethinking the Politics of Uncertainty*. London: Demos.

Preston-Shoot, M. (2001) 'Evaluating self-determination: an adult protection case study', *Journal of Adult Protection* 3: 4–14.

Prins, H. (1999) *Will They Do it Again?* London: Routledge.

Prins, H. (2005) *Offenders, Deviants or Patients?* London: Routledge.

Pritchard, J. (2008) 'Doing risk assessment properly in adult protection work', in J. Pritchard (ed.), *Good Practice in Safeguarding Adults: Working Effectively in Adult Protection*. London: Jessica Kingsley, pp. 191–233.

Reamer, F. (1983) 'Ethical dilemmas in social work practice', *Social Work* 28: 31–5.

Reamer, F. (2006) *Social Work Values and Ethics*, 3rd edn. New York: Columbia University Press.

Reason, J. (1997) *Managing the Risks of Organizational Accidents.* Aldershot: Ashgate.

Reason, J. (2008) *The Human Contribution: Unsafe Acts, Accidents and Heroic Recoveries.* Aldershot: Ashgate.

Reason, J. (2009) *The Human Contribution.* Aldershot: Ashgate.

Reder, P. and Duncan, S. (2004a) 'Making the most of the Victoria Climbié Inquiry Report', *Child Abuse Review* 13: 95–114.

Reder, P. and Duncan, S. (2004b) 'From Colwell to Climbié: inquiring into fatal child abuse', in J. Manthorpe and N. Stanley (eds), *The Age of the Inquiry.* London: Routledge, pp. 92–115.

Reder, P., Duncan, S. and Gray, M. (1993) *Beyond Blame: Child Abuse Tragedies Revisited.* London: Routledge.

Richards, S. (2000) 'Bridging the divide: elders and the assessment process', *British Journal of Social Work* 30: 37–49.

Risk Management Authority (2007) *Standards and Guidelines: Risk Management of Offenders Subject to an Order for Lifelong Restriction.* Paisley: Risk Management Authority.

Ritchie, J., Dick, D. and Lingham, R. (1994) *The Report of the Inquiry into the Care and Treatment of Christopher Clunis.* London: HMSO.

Roberts, J. and Hough, M. (2005) *Understanding Public Attitudes to Criminal Justice.* Maidenhead: Open University Press.

Robinson, G. and McNeill, F. (2008) 'Exploring the dynamics of compliance with community penalties', *Theoretical Criminology* 12: 431–49.

Robinson, L., de Benedictis, T. and Segal, J. (2012) 'Elder abuse and neglect: warning signs, risk factors, prevention, and help', www.helpguide.org/mental/elder_abuse_physical_emotional_sexual_neglect.htm#risk, accessed 3 March 2013.

Rochdale Borough Safeguarding Children's Board (2012) *Review of Multi-Agency Responses to the Sexual Exploitation of Children.* Available at www.rbscb.org/CSEReport.pdf, accessed 3 March 2013.

Rose, W. and Barnes, J. (2008) *Improving Safeguarding Practice: Study of Serious Case Reviews 2001–2003.* London: DCFS.

Russ, E., Lonne, B. and Darlington, Y. (2009) 'Using resilience to reconceptualise child protection workforce capacity', *Australian Social Work* 62: 324–38.

Schacter, D. (2001) *The Seven Sins of Memory: How the Mind Forgets and Remembers.* New York: Houghton Mifflin.

Schwalbe, C. (2004) 'Re-visioning risk assessment for human services decision making', *Children and Youth Services Review* 26: 561–76.

Schwalbe, C. (2008) 'A meta-analysis of juvenile justice risk assessment instruments: predictive validity by gender', *Criminal Justice and Behavior* 35: 1367–81.

Senge, P. (2006) *The Fifth Discipline: The Art and Practice of the Learning Organisation.* London: Random House Business Books.

Shardlow, S. (2002) 'Values, ethics and social work', in R. Adams, L. Dominelli and P. Malcolm (eds), *Social Work, Themes, Issues and Critical Debates*. Basingstoke: Palgrave, pp. 30–40.

Sheppard, D. (1996) *Learning the Lessons: Mental Health Inquiry Reports Published in England and Wales between 1969 and 1996 and their Recommendations for Improving Practice*. London: Zito Trust.

Sheppard, M. (2008) 'How important is prevention? High thresholds and outcomes for applicants refused by children's services: a six-month follow up', *British Journal of Social Work* 38: 1268–82.

Sidebotham, P., Brandon, M., Powell, C. et al. (2010) *Learning from Serious Case Reviews: Report of a Research Study on the Methods of Learning Lessons Nationally from Serious Case Reviews*. London: Department for Education.

Sinclair, R. and Bullock, R. (2002) *Learning from Past Experience – A Review of Serious Case Reviews*. London: Department of Health.

Slovic, P. (1986) 'Informing and educating the public about risk', *Risk Analysis* 6: 403–15.

Slovic, P. (1987) 'Perception of risk', *Science* 236: 280–5.

Slovic, P. (2000) *The Perception of Risk*. London: Earthscan.

Smale, G. and Tuson, G. with Biehal, N. and Marsh, P. (1993) *Empowerment, Assessment, Care Management and the Skilled Worker*. London: The Stationery Office.

Smith, M., McMahon, L. and Nursten, J. (2003) 'Social workers' experiences of fear', *British Journal of Social Work* 33: 659–71.

Stanley, N. and Manthorpe, J. (2001) 'Reading mental health inquiries: messages for social work', *Journal of Social Work* 1: 77–99.

Stanley, N. and Manthorpe, J. (2004) *The Age of the Inquiry: Learning and Blaming in Health and Social Care*. London: Routledge.

Stevens, M., Moriarty, J., Manthorpe, J., Hussein, S. (2010) 'Helping others or a rewarding career? Investigating student motivations to train as social workers in England', *Journal of Social Work* 12: 16–36.

Stevenson, O. (1999) 'Old people at risk', in P. Parsloe (ed.), *Risk Assessment in Social Care and Social Work*. London: Jessica Kingsley Publishers, pp. 201–16.

Strachan, R. and Tallant, C. (1997) 'Improving judgement and appreciating biases within the risk assessment process', in H. Kemshall and J. Pritchard (eds), *Good Practice in Risk Assessment and Risk Management*, vol. 2. London: Jessica Kingsley Publishers, pp. 15–26.

Straw, J. (1998) *Commons Sitting of 26 October 1998*. UK Parliament.

Tavris, C. and Aaronson, E. (2007) *Mistakes Were Made (But Not By Me): Why We Justify Foolish Beliefs, Bad Decisions and Hurtful Acts*. Orlando: Harcourt.

Taylor, B. (2006) 'Risk management paradigms in health and social services for professional decision making on the long-term care of older people', *British Journal of Social Work* 36: 1411–29.

Thomas, N. (2011) 'Care planning and review for looked after children: fifteen years of slow progress?', *British Journal of Social Work* 41: 387–98.

Thomson, A. (2000) 'Warning: you're risking death by being alive', *Daily Telegraph* (27 October): 21.

Tindall, B. (1997) 'People with learning difficulties: citizenship, personal development and the management of risk', in H. Kemshall and J. Pritchard (eds), *Good Practice in Risk Assessment and Risk Management*, vol. 2. London: Jessica Kingsley Publishers, pp. 103–17.

Titterton, M. (2005) *Risk and Risk Taking in Health and Social Welfare*. London: Jessica Kingsley Publishers.

Titterton, M. (2011) 'Positive risk taking with people at risk of harm', in H. Kemshall and B. Wilkinson (eds), *Good Practice in Assessing Risk: Current Knowledge, Issues and Approaches*. London: Jessica Kingsley, pp. 30–47.

Trevithick, P. (2000) *Social Work Skills: A Practice Handbook*. Buckingham: Open University Press.

Trotter, C. (2002) 'Worker skill and client outcome in child protection', *Child Abuse Review* 11: 38–50.

Tversky, A. and Kahneman, D. (1974) 'Judgement under uncertainty: heuristics and biases', *Science* 185: 1124–31.

Verita and Capsticks (2008) *A Review of 14 Mental Health Homicides Committed Between April 2002 and June 2006*. NHS East of England.

Webb, S. (2002) 'Evidence-based practice and decision analysis in social work: an implementation model', *Journal of Social Work* 2: 45–63.

Whyte, B. (2009) *Youth Justice in Practice*. Bristol: The Policy Press.

Wikström, P.-O. and Treiber, K. (2008) *Offending Behaviour Programmes: Source Document*. London: Youth Justice Board.

Wilkinson, B. (2011) 'Best practice in avoiding error', in H. Kemshall, G. Mackenzie, J. Miller and B. Wilkinson (eds), *Risk of Harm Guidance and Training Resources (Version 4.36)*. London: National Offender Management Service.

Wilson, S. (2009) 'Leading practice improvement in front line child protection', *British Journal of Social Work* 39: 64–80.

Women's Aid (2006) 'Who are the victims of domestic violence?', www. womensaid.org.uk/domestic-violence-articles.asp?section=00010001002 200410001&itemid=1273, accessed 1 March 2013.

World Health Organization (2002) *World Health Report on Violence and Health*. Geneva: World Health Organization.

# Index

abuse 13
  children *see* child abuse
  learning disabled people 79
  older people 13, 25–6, 27–9, 79
abusers
  care professionals as 115–16
  communicating with 36, 40–1,
    87
  emotions in decision
    making 58–9
  grading information sources 47,
    48, 50
  threats to social workers 118
accountability 160–1
actuarial/probability
    calculations 2–3, 21–2, 55,
    58, 68
administrative model
    interviews 38
agency-centred risk
    assessments 38
aggressive service users 66, 118,
    156
analysis, decision 67–9
analytical skills
  decision making 45, 52–8
  risk assessment 39–40
approach goals 87, 88, 89

assertive negotiation 117–18
assessment of risk *see* risk
    assessment
audit 134–6
Aukland, John George 50
autonomy 107, 110, 114–15, 117
availability bias 63, 66
aversion to risk 118
avoidance goals 87, 88
avoidance of risk *see* risk
    avoidance

Bain, A. 60
Baker, K. 88
Bandura, A. 151–2
Banks, S. 103
beliefs
  biased 65
  ethical 107–9
  self-efficacy 150–2, 162
biases, decision making 50–2,
    63–6
black and minority ethnic (BME)
    communities 79
Bostock, L. 137–8
British Association of Social
    Workers (BASW) 101, 110,
    111, 112–13, 115

Calder, M. 143
Carson, D. 60
case records *see* records
caseloads 125
categorization 73–4, 98
certainty/first impression
  bias 50–2
change strategies 75, 82–8, 89,
  93, 169
change targets 75, 78–82, 169
child abuse 13
  by care professionals 115–16
  categorization 73–4
  communication 36–7, 40–1, 87,
    124
  critical reasoning 52–5
  emotions in decision
    making 58–9
  grading information sources 47,
    48, 50–1
  manipulation of social
    workers 118
  'near misses' 137
  risk assessment 14, 36–7,
    40–1
  risk factors 24–5
  risk management 72–3, 76–7,
    87, 94
  risk scenarios 68
  thresholds 72–3
child neglect 13
  critical reasoning 52–5
  'near misses' 137, 138
  risk assessment 14
  risk management 72–3, 84–5,
    89–91
  thresholds 72–3
child protection
  categorization 73–4
  critical incident reporting 136,
    137
  critical reasoning 52–5
  emotions in decision
    making 58–9, 157
  grading information sources 47,
    48, 50–1

learning from inquiries/
  SCRs 123, 125
learning from 'near
  misses' 137–8
multi-agency
  communication 33–4, 94
  risk management 76–7, 84–5,
    87, 89–91, 94
  risk scenarios 68, 94
  risks posed to children 4
routinization 43
service-user communication 36,
  40–1, 87
Stockholm syndrome 118
thresholds 72–3
children
  abuse of *see* child abuse
  neglect of *see* child neglect
  protection *see* child protection
  risk assessment 13, 14
    balanced practice 15, 16–18
    causal patterns 26–7
    communication in 33–4,
      36–7, 40–1
    impacts of risk 14, 26–7, 34
    individual attributes for 40–1
    risk factors 24–5
    structured tools 22
  risk management 72–3, 76–7,
    84–5, 87, 89–91, 92, 94
clients *see* service users
Climbié, Victoria 124, 125
Common Assessment Framework
  (CAF) 22
communication 32–9
  professional–professional 32–5,
    40, 97–9, 124
  professional–service user 35–9,
    40–1, 87, 117–18, 124
  recorded information 40, 96–7
compromise 118–19
confirmation bias 64, 66
conflict management 40–1
consent 33
contingency planning 75, 93–5
coping skills 153, 159–60, 171

criminal offenders
    decision making   46, 47, 58–9,
        64
    ethical dilemmas   105, 106, 110
    risk management   83, 86–7
critical incident reporting   136–8
critical questions   138–40
critical reasoning   45–50, 51–8
critical reflection *see* self-awareness
        and reflection
cultural contexts
    abuse by care professionals
        116
    learning   143, 144, 154, 171
    risk management   79

dangerous and severe personality
        disorder (DSPD)   105, 106
Darlington, Y.   154
data, for review of risk
        work   134–5
decision making   5, 43–69, 167–8
    biases   50–2, 63–6
    case priorities   112
    compromise   118
    critical reasoning   45–50, 51–8
    decision analysis   67–9
    defensible   19–20
    emotions   57, 58–9, 157
    evidence weighing   50–2
    in groups   98–9
    knowledge for   46, 49–50,
        149–50
    option balancing   59–63, 67–9,
        168–9
    precautionary principle   44, 63
    reflection   55–8, 154, 157
    review *see* review of risk work
    risk scenario rehearsing   67–9
    routinization   43–4
    self-management   146, 153, 154,
        157, 160–1
    service-user involvement   14–15,
        17, 18–19, 55
    skills for   44–58
    supervision   160–1

thresholds   29, 72–3, 74
    values   59–63, 68, 69
defensible practice   19–20
Department for Children, Schools
        and Families (DCSF)   13,
        14, 123
disabled people   18, 79
discrimination   65
domestic violence   26–7, 52–5
Downham, G.   126–7
dread risks   58–9

economic stress   26, 27
efficacy, personal   150–2, 162
elder abuse
    risk factors for   25–6, 27–9, 79
    risk planning   79
    WHO definition   13
emotion-focused coping   153
emotional abuse   13, 14
emotions
    decision making and   57, 58–9,
        157
    self-management   154–6, 157
empowerment   18–19
ethics   7, 101–19, 170
    abuse by social workers
        115–16
    codes   103, 110, 111, 112–13,
        115
    common issues   101–3, 119
    compromise   118–19
    lying to service users   114–15
    manipulation of service
        users   113–14, 117
    professional integrity   113
    resource rationing   111–12
    risks–rights tension   104–6,
        109–11
    role boundaries   112–19
    social workers' values   103–4,
        106, 107–9, 112–13
    whistle-blowing   113, 116
evaluation of risk practice *see*
        review of risk work
exchange model interviews   38

false negative risk decisions 29, 72
false positive risk decisions 29, 72
fear, of clients 66, 118, 156
financial abuse 13
first impression bias 50–2
footsteps to change 93
Francis, R. Q. C. 104

George, Vanessa 115–16
goals 75–8, 87–8, 89
groups, decision making 98–9
guidance, professional 23

Her Majesty's Inspectorate of Probation (HMIP) 83
heuristics 54, 56
hindsight bias 63
human rights
  multi-agency communication 33
  risks–rights tension 104–6, 109–11
hypotheses 56–7, 168

iceberg model 157, 158
impacts of risk 14, 26–7, 29, 34
information
  analysis in risk assessment 39–40
  communication in risk assessment 32–5, 40, 124
  critical appraisal 45–50, 51–8
  grading sources of 47–9, 50–1
  recording in risk assessment 40
  testing chains of 135, 136
inquiries 123–31
insurance industry 2–3
Integrated Children's System (ICS) 22
integrity 113, 148–9
interagency working *see* multi-agency working
interpersonal skills 155–6

interpretive repertoires 98
interviews 35–9, 87
intrapersonal skills 155–6
intuitive reasoning 54, 56–7

Jarvis, Christopher 115
judgement, exercising sound 45–52
*see also* decision making

Kelly, G. 88
knowledge 46, 49–50, 149–50

learning 121, 122–3
  from inquiries/SCRs 123–31
  risk systems 136–8, 142–3, 144
  self-management 150, 159, 160–1, 162–3
learning-disabled people 79
legislation
  communication shaped by 33
  ethical dilemmas 105, 106, 110–11
  *see also* rules for practice
Lingham, R. 126–7
Lonne, B. 154
lying to service users 114–15

'making do', ethics of 111–12
male service users, communication 35–6
management of self *see* self-management
managing risk *see* risk-management planning
material abuse 13
means–end thinking 89, 90–1
meetings 98–9
mentally ill persons
  communication 124
  dual nature of risk in 4–5
  risk factors for violence by 24
  risk management 76, 86, 87
mistakes 57
  critical incident reporting 136
  'near misses' 136–8

monitoring   134, 135, 136–40,
      142
motivation, social workers   148–9
multi-agency working
   communication   32–5, 40, 124
   skills in   97–9, 169
   training for   125
Munro, E.   57, 68–9

National Council on Independent
      Living (NCIL)   18
'near misses'   136–8
need(s), definition   18
neglect
   of children *see* child neglect
   definition of in older people   13
negotiation, assertive   117–18
nurseries, child abuse
      within   115–16
Nuttall, Lawrence   106

offenders *see* criminal offenders
older people
   categorization   74
   ethics   107
   grading information
      sources   48–9
   risk assessment   13, 15, 25–6,
      27–9
   risk factors for abuse of   25–6,
      27–9, 79
   risk management   79, 80, 87, 92
   WHO definition of abuse/
      neglect   13
optimism   64, 65, 138
organizational learning   122–31,
      136–8, 143, 154
organizational risk systems *see* risk
      systems
organizational skills   31–2
organizations, self-management
      in   146–64, 171
outcomes
   decision making   59–63, 67–9
   risk assessment   14–15
   risk management   75–7

paradigms, risk-management   98
participatory practice   87
peer relationships   159–60
peer review   159
personal risk, social policy   3
personality disorder   104–5, 106
personalization   18–19
pessimism   65
physical abuse, WHO
      definition   13
   *see also* child abuse; elder abuse
planning for risk *see* risk-
      management planning
poverty   26
power
   abuse by social workers   115
   communication and   33, 35–6,
      37, 124
   manipulation of service
      users   113–14
   personalization agenda   18–19
   risk-management
      strategies   83–4
precautionary principle   44, 63
prevention of risk
   confusion with protection   18
   ethics   105, 106
preventive detention   105, 106
principles, rules and   23, 24
   *see also* ethics, codes
privacy rights   33
probability/actuarial
      calculations   2–3, 21–2, 55,
      58, 68
problem-solving coping   153
professional guidance   23
professional integrity   113, 148–9
professional–professional
      communication   32–5, 40,
      97–9, 124
   *see also* peer relationships
professional–service user
      communication   35–9,
      40–1, 87, 117–18, 124
professional standards, risk policies
      as   132–3

proportionality 110–11
protection from risk 18–19
children *see* child protection
protective factors 27, 28–9
*see also* resilience factors
psychological/emotional abuse 13,
14

quality assurance 131, 134–6
questioning
difficult questions 138–40
in interviews 37, 38, 87

records
risk-assessment 40, 96, 169
risk-management 75, 95–7, 169
reflection on practice *see* self-
awareness and reflection
reports, inquiry/SCR 123–31
representative bias 64, 66
resilience, social workers 152–4,
159–60, 163
resilience factors, assessment 46
*see also* protective factors;
strengths
resources 125
rationing 111–12
responsibility–risk relation 3
review of risk work 7, 121–44,
170
audit 134–6
communication 124
critical questions 138–40
inquiries/SCRs 123–31
learning systems 136–8, 142–3,
144
monitoring 134, 135, 136–40,
142
'near misses' 136–8
quality assurance 131, 134–6
report
recommendations 126–31
resources 125
responsibility for 121
risk assessment 125
risk policies 132–4

risk system oversight 140–1,
144, 170
staff training 125
supervision 125, 130
rights *see* human rights
risk
defining 1–3
in social work 3–8
risk assessment 2–5, 6, 9–41,
167–8
actuarial 21–2
balanced practice 10–11, 15–19
categorization arising
from 73–4
causal patterns 26–9
communication in 32–9, 40–1
decision making *see* decision
making
defensible practice 19–20
individuals in context 13–15
learning from inquiries 125
meaning 11
'near misses' 137
organization for 31–2
policy contexts 17–18
protective factors 27, 28–9
purpose 11–12
records 40, 96, 169
reflection 30–1, 38–9, 40–1,
55–6
review *see* review of risk work
risk factors 21–2, 24–9
risk management and 71, 72–4
*see also* risk-management
planning
self-awareness 30–1, 38–9,
40–1
self-management skills 157
service-user involvement 14–15,
17, 18–19, 55
skills for 9–11, 19–20, 29–41
social contexts 18, 25, 26
structured tools 22–3
thresholds 29, 72–3, 74
unstructured 20–1
working positively 170–1

risk avoidance  44
  balance with positive risk
      taking  10–11, 18–19, 74
  categorization  74
  emotions in decision making  59
  ethics  118
risk controllers  131, 140–1
risk decisions *see* decision making
risk enablement  10, 18, 74
risk factors  21–2, 24–9
  causal links  26–9, 63, 80–2
  critical reasoning exercise  52–3,
      54
  knowledge of essential  49–50
  knowledge needed to assess  46
  risk-management
      planning  78–82, 93–4
risk impacts  14, 26–7, 29, 34
risk-management planning  6–7,
      71–100, 168–9
  change strategies  75, 82–8, 89,
      93, 169
  change targets  75, 78–82, 169
  contextual information  78–9
  contingency planning  75, 93–5
  ethics  117–18
  goals  75–8, 87–8, 89
  records  75, 95–7, 169
  review  75, 95
      *see also* review of risk work
  risk-assessment and  71, 72–4
  risk categorization  73–4
  role clarification  71–2, 87
  scenario planning  94–5
  sequencing  75, 88–93
  thresholds  72–3, 74
  timescales  75, 88–93
  urgency  89
  working with others  97–9, 169
  working positively  170–1
risk policies  132–4
risk practice review *see* review of
      risk work
risk prevention  18, 105, 106
risk protection  18–19
  children *see* child protection

risk reduction  14–15
risk scenarios  67–9, 94–5
risk systems  131–43, 144, 170
  audit  134–6
  learning  136–8, 142–3, 144
  monitoring  134, 135, 136–40,
      142
  oversight  140–1
  quality assurance  131, 134–6
  risk policies  132–4
risk taking, positive
  risk assessment  10–11, 14–15,
      18–19
  risk-management planning  74,
      78, 79, 117–18
Ritchie, Anne  55–6
Robinson, Andrew  4–5, 124
role boundaries  112–19
role clarification  71–2, 87
routinization, risk decisions  43–4
rules for practice  23, 24
  *see also* legislation
rumination  157, 163
Russ, E.  154

scenario planning  94–5
scenario rehearsing  67–9
self-awareness and reflection
  biases  64–6
  in decision making  55–8, 59,
      62–3, 64–6, 154, 157
  emotions  59, 157
  ethical beliefs  107
  in risk assessment  30–1, 38–9,
      40–1
  in self-management  149, 150–1,
      154, 157
self-efficacy  150–2, 162
self-management  7, 146–64, 171
  critical reflection skills  149,
      150–1
  emotions  154–6, 157
  knowledge  149–50
  learning opportunities  162–3
  motivation  148–9
  risk and  157–8

self-efficacy beliefs 150–2,
162
stress 146, 152–4, 159–60,
163
supervision 160–2, 171
working with peers 159–60
work–life balance 163
sequencing, risk management 75,
88–93
serious case reviews
(SCRs) 123–31
service users
abuse by social workers
115–16
assertive negotiation 117–18
biases about 65–6
communicating with 35–9,
40–1, 87, 117–18, 124
decision-making
involvement 14–15, 17,
18–19, 55
grading information from 47,
48–9
lying to 114–15
manipulation by social
workers 113–14, 117
manipulation of social
workers 118
organizational responses to
SCRs 128, 129
practitioners' emotions 155–6,
157
risk-management
involvement 74, 77–8,
82–8, 89, 93, 117–18
risks–rights tension 104–6,
109–11
sexual abuse, WHO definition
13
sexual abuse of children
by care professionals 115–16
categorization 73–4
emotions in decision
making 58–9
'near misses' 137
risk management 76–7

sexual abuse of learning disabled
people 79
skills
decision-making 44–58
risk-assessment 9–11, 19–20,
29–41
self-management 147–56
working with others 97–9,
169
Slovic, P. 58
social contexts
risk assessment 18, 25, 26
risk factors for child abuse 25
statutory supervision 110–11
Stockholm syndrome 118
Stone, Michael 104–5, 106
strengths
reflection on practitioners'
30–1
risk-assessment 14–15, 17, 27
risk-management 78, 79–80,
81–2, 84–5
see also resilience factors
stress
economic 26, 27
social workers 146, 152–4,
159–60, 163
structured assessment tools 22–3
supervision 125, 130, 160–2, 171
systems see risk systems

thinking
means–end 89, 90–1
social workers' patterns 154–5,
157, 158, 163
thresholds 29, 72–3, 74
timescales, risk management 75,
88–93
Titterton, M. 60–2, 108, 117
training, staff 125, 162–3

values
decision-making 59–63, 68, 69
ethical dilemmas 103–4, 106,
107–9, 112–13
organizational 132

violence
  against learning disabled
    people  79
  domestic  26–7, 52–5
  risk of in the mentally ill  24, 86
vulnerability to risk  4–5

Webb, S.  67
welfare state, risk attitudes  3

whistle-blowing  113, 116
Wilkinson, B.  88
work–life balance  163
World Health Organization
  (WHO)  13

young people
  categorization  73–4
  offender management  46, 83